Christian Education Made Easy

Strategies and Teaching Aids for Building a Strong Program in Any Size Church

A Companion to *Creative Christian Education*

Howard Hanchey

MOREHOUSE PUBLISHING
HARRISBURG, PENNSYLVANIA

Copyright © 1989 by Howard Hanchey

Morehouse Publishing
Harrisburg, Pennsylvania

Library of Congress Cataloging-in-Publication Data

Hanchey, Howard.
    Christian education made easy: strategies and teaching aids to build a strong Sunday school in any sized church/ Howard Hanchey.
        p.   cm.
    "A companion for Creative Christian education."
    Bibliography: p.
    ISBN 0-8192-1446-9
    1. Christian education. 2. Sunday-schools.
I. Hanchey, Howard. Creative Christian education.
II. Title.
BV1471.2.H373   1989   88-38710
268'.83—dc19   CIP

Printed in the United States of America
by
BSC LITHO
Harrisburg, PA

10 9 8 7 6 5 4 3 2 1

Dedication

To the saints of God,
those faithful Sunday school teachers who,
through their love and because of their ministry,
from generation to generation,
provide the steady driving,
earthly engine that powers the
Church of God.

Contents

Contents   ix

Contents xiii

Acknowledgments

I want to thank those many people around this country who send me clippings and notes about the good results they've obtained by using approaches suggested in *Creative Christian Education*. A few of their stories and comments appear in the following pages. But if in the following pages you find something objectionable, I want to assure you that they had nothing at all to do with it.

Also, I am grateful to Gretchen Wolff Pritchard, dedicated Christian educator and editor of *The Sunday Paper*, whose work is cited in the Appendix A, and in the endnotes of chapter 2, for permission to use several of her drawings that once appeared in *The Living Church*.

Unless otherwise noted, Scripture quotations are my own translations, from the Greek or Hebrew text.

Illustrations

Preface

If you are a member of a small church who has given up on having a Sunday morning program of Christian education; or

—IF you are a member of a congregation of more than a thousand people, and you worry because a lot of different programs and activities generate too much busyness and too little soul-satisfying community; or

—IF you are tired of year after year shopping for expensive, store-bought curriculum materials, and somehow you have the feeling that things could be simpler; or

—IF you'd like to use the Bible more but don't know how to make this formidable book more manageable (after all, you only have about thirty-plus minutes in the Sunday morning classroom); or

—IF you are a first-time teacher excited by some of the ideas proposed in my book *Creative Christian Education* (Wilton, CT: Morehouse-Barlow, 1986), and now you want help in making specific plans; or

—IF you are a member of clergy, and you want to support your teachers with the kind of help you know you don't have the time or training to give; or

—IF you grew up in a Sunday school that didn't work for you, and because you want better for yourself and your children today, you're looking for a model that works;

then the following chapters will open perspectives you may have dreamed about on your best days but never had the courage (or encouragement) to develop.

Christian Education Made Easy (CEME) is written with several constituencies in mind. For those of you who have never taught in the Sunday school before, welcome. You will find in the following pages help with setting a goal and a few objectives for the year, encouragement to make use of, among other things, stories of God's action in the Bible, and more than a few ideas to help make whatever you study as satisfying as possible. As a result, your confidence will strengthen.

For Sunday school superintendents and clergy with an interest in or responsibility for Sunday morning Christian education, *CEME* offers both a vision and the practical helps to make easy the organization of your parish for education on Sunday morning. Work sheets are included to help your teachers make the kinds of plans that generate enthusiasm and confidence.

Christian education in small churches (less than one hundred members of all ages) is also an interest of mine. I grew up in rural America, and I know the way in which large church Sunday school programs set a model for Christian education that disables the vision needed to develop small church programs. Chapter 2 describes a method to organize a Sunday school program in a parish with only three or four children and a couple of interested adults, an approach used successfully in a number of small congregations.

The plain fact is this: No matter what the size of your Sunday school, if you give a bit of elbow grease and old-fashioned enthusiasm to the task of Sunday morning Christian education (as conceived in *CEME*), you will come close to constructing the kind of program about which you have always dreamed.

The four chapters in Part I of *CEME* present an overview of Sunday morning Christian education and what this book offers in response. Part II illustrates the easy way Bible stories can provide the bulk of curriculum materials—and it offers several ready-to-use plans for specific Bible stories. Part III presents specific guidelines to construct a successful Sunday morning program. And Part IV shows how five seasonal terms, first presented in *Creative Christian Education*, can be used to make your Sunday school program as full and creative as you have ever imagined it could be.

Also included are easy-to-use work sheets to help you
—set a goal and some objectives for your Sunday morning program,
—plan the full nine month year,
—plan each of the five suggested terms,
—plan every Sunday, and
—troubleshoot your program according to the size of your church.

These work sheets are designed to be photocopied, and since this book, when opened, approximates an 8½ by 11 inch sheet of paper, if the work sheet is copied by a machine capable of increasing the copy size by 154 percent, as many machines can do, the work sheet can be moved to a larger, 8½ by 14 inch sheet of paper.

If you need more help than this book can offer, you can find assistance at the Center for the Ministry of Teaching (CMT) at the Virginia Theological Seminary, in Alexandria, VA 22304. CMT can be reached through the seminary switchboard, 1-703-370-6600. Tell the CMT staff that you need advice on curriculum resources, and they will answer every one of your questions with practical suggestions. They enjoy being helpful, and their ministry is one of serving the Church.

When you identify a book or resource that you need, and particularly if you can't find it locally, it can be purchased through the Seminary Book Service of the Virginia Theological Seminary. This book service can also be reached through the seminary switchboard, or better, use its toll free number, 800-368-3756. A list of the books I often use in my plans for Sunday morning Christian education is found in the Appendix A, A Bookstore For You.

But if you telephone the Seminary Book Service, don't forget to mention that you are calling because of this note in *Christian Education Made Easy.* We're always trying to figure out how we can better serve Christian education in the Church.

And if I can be of help, please give me a telephone call. Use the Virginia Theological Seminary switchboard to reach me. If I'm not in the office or if I'm in class, I'll be happy to call you back on your nickel, and if I can't answer your question to my satisfaction, I'll probably refer you to CMT. Also, along with the staff of CMT, I am often asked to prepare and present Christian education workshops. If we can help you in this way, just ask.

Sunday morning Christian education is the most exciting and the most fundamental ministry in the church, and the following pages show why.

The Virginia Theological Seminary   H.H.
Alexandria, Virginia
February 1, 1989

PART I

Catching the Vision

CHAPTER ONE

Making Plans For Success

"I don't know what to do; there are so many materials available," an exhausted Sunday school superintendent sighed. "We don't know which one to choose, they're expensive, and none of them quite does what we want."

"Why not custom make your own program" said I, to which she rejoined, "I wouldn't even know where to begin."

I do know where to begin, and this book is devoted to helping you see the same thing. The plain fact is this: the task of creating a unique-to-your-church Sunday morning program is easy and fun, whether you decide to start from scratch or simply adapt ready-made materials to your particular setting. More, creating or adapting curricula materials builds teacher enthusiasm, and it generates parish esprit de corps, and *Christian Education Made Easy (CEME)* provides an easy-to-use seven-step procedure to make this task smooth and agreeable. Chapter 2 shows this plan in action in a small church setting.

But even if you're using store-bought curricula materials, the ideas in *CEME* can relate your ready-made curriculum more directly to the weekly life of your parish.

Basically this is what you will find in the following pages:

1. A high value placed on God's ministry, and the ways and means to help both children and adults meet and be met by God.

2. The importance of, and the ways and means to develop a goal and set a few objectives for your nine month long program.

3. A way to "shorten" the nine month long year by dividing it into five terms of study, and using teaching teams to spread the responsibility.

4. The ways and means to make Christian education a celebration by involving the whole parish in it, and by celebrating classroom learning with term-ending jubilee, show-and-tell festivals.

5. The importance of an easy way to use just a few Bible stories every year, and by a few I mean just four or five. Less is actually more when we consider that many of us have only thirty-plus minutes with which to work on Sunday morning, and the study of a few Bible stories every year feeds a hunger that many Christians want assuaged.

When Sunday morning Christian education goes well, everything else in the parish follows suit. The following pages are designed with your success in mind.

Now some of my colleagues criticize the word success in this chapter's title. They say it makes Christian education "too commercial."

POINT. But the plain fact is this; in my travels around the church I hear a heartfelt wish to make Sunday morning Christian education successful. People are fed up with failure, and they are tired of just limping along. "There must be a better way," they think, and they're equally tired of spending large sums every year for the latest ready-made, store-bought materials, only to find out that something invariably goes wrong.[1]

More, I have found that when Sunday school goes well, the life of the parish follows suit. A strong Sunday school contributes to a strong and vital congregational life, and an increasing number of congregations are discovering this point. Hence, every year more and more congregations are creating their own "home grown" programs. Still others are "customizing" their store-bought materials using ideas like those found in this book. Around the church confidence is accelerating, and if you're now thinking about joining this parade, *CEME* is designed to encourage your interest and make you confident.

But maybe you're still apprehensive about designing your own curricula materials. I want to assure you that although the task is a bit harder than simply using off-the-shelf materials, when you buy a ready-made program, at least some of what you sacrifice is the joy of colleagues working together on a task they love and building a program that fits your church to a *T*. More, teachers working together mark every successful Sunday morning program.

If you're already using ready-made curricula, the ideas in *CEME* can make your materials work even better. For example, do you know how the size of your congregation dictates what you can reasonably expect from Sunday morning Christian education? If you find yourself now interested in this discussion or this issue, see chapter 11 in *CEME*. Are you aware of the importance of setting a few reasonable objectives every year, and have you considered occasional show-and-tell festivals to celebrate what you are learning in the classroom? Each of the following sections, which describe *CEME's* seven-step plan, lists ideas you may wish to try.

Finally, if you're shopping for a ready-made program, *CEME* suggests that before you purchase, you evaluate the materials from the following perspectives:

1. How do these materials manage the nine-month school year? Are there terms or blocks of study with discrete foci, or does the program drag on and on for nine months?

2. Does the program encourage teacher initiative and consultation with one another, or is it so skillfully packaged that teachers end up working in isolation all through the year?

3. Does it make use of the Bible, and if it does not, how does it propose that we learn of God's action in the past, so that we can more easily identify God's action in our lives today?

4. Does this program encourage your parish to set a goal for the year and identify and formulate a few easy-to-accomplish objectives?

5. Does it provide opportunities, along with the ways and means, to celebrate before the parish what is happening in the Sunday morning classroom? Parents like to know what their children are learning, and occasional parish celebrations not only "bless" the children, they satisfy parents and affirm teachers. With this kind of atmosphere it's not difficult to fill the ranks of teachers year after year.

CLAIMING SUCCESS

If by now I've elicited your interest, you'll want to know that *CEME* is divided into four parts to make your planning easy. Part I presents the ways and means to easily organize the lengthy and often forbidding nine-month teaching year, a far easier task than many first suspect. These organizing principles were first presented in the first three chapters of my book *Creative Christian Education* (published by Morehouse-Barlow in 1986).

The second part of *CEME* develops and demonstrates an easy-to-use method of Bible Study. Let's face it, the Bible is the most important resource available for Christian education.

Finally, the third and fourth parts of *CEME* provide all the tools necessary to make plans to implement your newly found ideas, and set some reasonable objectives to make your dreams real. In particular, the chapters in Part IV note specific study possibilities for every age group;

—children (preschool through grade seven),

—teenagers, and

—adults.

In summary, *Christian Education Made Easy (CEME)* provides the ways and means to construct a successful, homegrown Sunday school program in any sized church. It can stand on its own, but it is also designed and written to work as a companion with *Creative Christian Education.*

GETTING STARTED

I've been involved in some form of Christian education all my life, and I know this book's subject backward and forward.

I spent a part of every childhood year in the Sunday morning classroom, and later I taught there as well. I'm now an Episcopal priest. I've served several parishes as rector, and at present I am a seminary professor. In my adult years, I'm the father of two daughters who have attended, and now occasionally teach in the Sunday morning classroom. I'm also the husband of a fourth-grade teacher who enjoys leading both adults and children as together they journey toward the maturation of faith. An interest in Christian education is never distant from this family's life.

When I wrote *Creative Christian Education*, I said that there were five components in every program of successful Christian education:

—The nine month school year had to be broken into manageable parts,

—Christian education needed to be treated as a celebration,

—the Bible needed to have an important place in whatever written curriculum was used,

—the more everyone in the parish was involved, the more likely the program was to be successful, and

—God's ministry has to be valued as the primary ministry it is.

These component parts are still necessary for success. My thinking has not changed one bit.

But with the help of educators and teachers across America, I've also discovered that four more factors also deserve special attention. Each one is developed in this chapter and the chapters that follow.

First, Christian education must be valued as mission, and what I have learned to call a mission perspective nearly always fuels successful programs. "So what is this mission perspective?" you ask. A mission perspective above all else rejoices in the study of God, not abstract ideas about God, but God in action in both Scripture and life today. Part II of *CEME* presents and demonstrates several easy-to-use tools that make Bible study easy, and each one is designed to work in the few brief minutes available in the Sunday morning classroom.

Now if you're already familiar with *Creative Christian Education*, you know this mission perspective is simply another expression of my first book's close attention to valuing the study of God's ministry, whether God's ministry is found in the Bible or in the here-and-now of life today. The plain fact is this: I've been heartened to see (over and over again) that when the study of God's ministry is valued in the Sunday morning classroom, Christian education becomes a celebration marked with success.

Second, a mission perspective is energized by the study of Bible stories, but what I did not realize when I wrote *Creative Christian Education* is this: Many teachers have learned to fear the use of Scripture in the Sunday morning classroom, even though Bible stories are a splendid and basic resource for Christian education. So often left out of Sunday morning Christian education is an aggressive use of the Bible and its stories. *CEME* addresses this issue head on and provides both the perspectives and the tools to make Bible study satisfying and fun.

Third, successful programs of Christian education pay careful attention to the development of a goal for the year, and they set before the whole parish a few realistic learning objectives. For example, before the year begins it is far better to decide that "This year we want to learn about God" (a goal), and set as objectives the exploration of four or five Bible stories during the next nine months (recognizing that we have only thirty-plus minutes with which to work on Sunday morning), than it is to study the whole Bible, remember almost nothing and leave the parish with an unsatisfactory taste in its corporate mouth.

We need to learn afresh that "less is actually more" when making plans for the Sunday morning classroom, and setting a goal and a few realistic objectives goes a long way toward insuring the implementation of this good notion.

Fourth, I also learned that the size of a congregation makes a difference in Sunday morning Christian education. Big and small churches have different needs, and small churches often feel like they're too small to have a "good" Sunday school. *CEME* pays special attention to small church Christian education and devotes a full chapter (chapter 2) to organizing a small church program from scratch.

USING *CEME*'s SEVEN-STEP PLAN

If by now you're more than a little interested in developing your own homegrown curriculum, the following seven steps, introduced in this chapter and explained more fully in succeeding chapters, will ensure your success and offer all the help you'll need.

1. Right from the beginning *recognize that Christian education is mission, a mission committed to telling the world about God.* Call this first step "developing your attitude about Christian education."

2. To learn of godly things, prepare to *have fun with a few Bible stories every year.* The use of Bible stories brings the mission perspective to life, and this second step encourages you to include at least a bit of Bible study in your yearly plans.

3. But in addition to Bible stories, *be prepared to use the wealth of other materials listed in Part IV of CEME,* such as the way we help God take care of God's world (a study of sainthood during the All Saints term), along with investigations of parish history, baptism and/or the Lord's Holy Communion. With these many possibilities it doesn't take long to fill up a year or a six week term.

4. *Manage nine months creatively* by breaking the year into five terms, and conclude each term with a show-and-tell festival. This fourth step values the management of the church year. By this point in your planning you have content in hand, the ways and means to manage it for nine months, and some concrete ideas about making Christian education a celebration.

5. *Determine a goal and set a few objectives* for the year. Next publish them for all in the parish. This is where many Christian education programs go wrong; no one has much of an idea about what the Sunday morning program is trying to accomplish. A goal goes a long way toward making Christian education sound more like a symphony than a noise, and step five is designed to help you put

a goal and a few objectives together. Part III of *CEME* shows you how to do both, and along with helpful work sheets this section reminds you that when planning Sunday morning Christian education, "less is always more."

(6.) Step six encourages you to keep the public school model of education in its place, the public school. *Don't be intimidated or confused by the public school model of education.* Every week public and private school educators have up to thirty classroom hours with which to work with their students, while we have thirty-plus minutes. The public school can do things about which we can only dream, and when parents "complain" about our not doing more, invite them to consider our limitations as well as their "at home" responsibilities.

You might also want to value more deeply the important "other" ways that Christian education is taking place in your church on Sunday morning; in worship—paying particular attention to the inclusion of young children in the eucharist (see chapter 3), when we fellowship at the coffee-hour, when we greet one another at the door, and the witness that our presence on Sunday morning makes to one another.

(7.) Finally, be aware of the *danger of depending too much on store-bought curriculum materials,* how easy it is to succumb to the "lazy" temptations they offer, and how teacher morale often suffers as a result.

Thinking out loud about using this seven step plan, one diocesan Christian educator anticipates this scenario.

> I would envision the education staff and planners sitting down in the late winter and early spring to read through parts I, II, and III of *CEME* for the vision and concept that it poses, begin to formulate a goal and set a few objectives for the year, and still later use parts III and IV to make specific teaching plans for each of the five terms.
>
> Then when these plans are published in September, what is set for the year would no longer be a secret, which it is in too many instances, and don't parish programs suffer when this happens?
>
> I would also see that prior to each of the five terms, teaching teams and Sunday school administrators would meet to fine-tune specific plans, paying particular attention to the development of the show-and-tell festivals.[2]

Step One: Recognize that Christian Education is Mission

Right off the bat we must recognize that in both the church and in the world there is a deep yearning to know more about the things of God, not less.

People want to know who God is and how God acts, they want practical insights into the difference that God makes in their lives, and they want Sunday morning Christian education to pay attention to these longings.

Hence, successful Christian education programs make every effort to answer the questions these hungry folks ask. Mission-minded programs love to celebrate God's presence and ministry in the world, they love to talk about it, they love to teach about it and they find every possible support in their use of Bible stories.

If you want a gang buster Sunday morning program, celebrate God's presence and ministry by using Bible stories. Explore God's ministry through drama and play, picture God's action in classroom-made banners, and by using a few crafts and other activities to draw out the Bible story you're studying, God will strengthen the Christian faith of each and every participant. You can count on it.

Because this mission perspective is such an important concept, let me discuss it in more detail.

There are two fundamental mind-sets in every Christian congregation. One is a *mission mind-set* and the other is a *maintenance mind-set*. Both are necessary, but in Sunday morning Christian education the mission mind-set breathes life while the maintenance mind-set breeds disappointment.

As you might expect, a church with a maintenance mind-set is primarily a task-centered church. Leadership in this congregation spends much of its time worrying about maintenance and conservation. "The parish hall needs a new roof," says the buildings and grounds committee, "The Sunday school needs a new curriculum to work well," another says, "We have got to have a more successful stewardship drive this year," says still another, or "We've got to be more socially involved in the community." There are a lot of "oughts" and "shoulds" in maintenance-minded congregations and programs.

A mission perspective, on the other hand, embodies a first-century Christian spirit. Think of the bold-hearted life present in early Christian congregations. Jesus was only a few decades raised from the dead, word of Paul's ministry was filtering through the church in bits and pieces, and even for Christians distant from the Palestinian roads that Jesus walked, every once in a while someone who had known Jesus in the flesh came near. These early Christians lived on the edge of eternity, and their lives were fired with expectation. Someone great had touched their lives, and something great had happened in the world. God was near, and they knew it.

Mission-minded Christian education taps this ancient gospel

theme. These programs know that it is more than a fairy tale that God is doing infinitely more in our midst than we can ask for or imagine (Eph. 3:20). Now make no mistake; mission-minded education is concerned with tasks like feeding the poor and caring for the oppressed. But more, mission-minded education centers its attention first of all on God and God's action in the world, knowing full well that when celebrating God's presence and ministry is the first order of business, all else falls into place.

POINT. Maintenance-minded Christian education, on the other hand, tends toward an obsession with getting the right curricula materials, making sure children behave, making sure children and adults come to Sunday school and, with so much attention to tasks, ends up missing the spirit of the Christian enterprise. There's a better way.

To help a mission perspective take a firm shape in your parish educational program, don't miss any opportunity to spend whatever time is necessary before the year begins to develop a goal and several objectives for the year, and in both your goal and the objectives you pose include a celebration and study of God's ministry. Such a goal might sound something like this:

> To make believers out of Christians, by having fun with Bible stories and other traditional things.

Or your goal might sound like this:

> To enjoy the task of meeting God and getting to know God through the use of Bible stories.

Chapter 12 is designed to help you with the task of developing a mission-minded goal and setting a few objectives for the year.

Step Two: Have Fun with Bible Stories

Mission-minded Christian education knows that the Bible is the best of all books to use in the Sunday morning classroom. Faith is transmitted, not because facts are memorized (as facts are often learned and memorized in the public school), but because generation after generation chooses to celebrate Bible stories of God's action. Through this celebration God chooses to say to us "I'm true."

POINT. When Bible stories are used and enjoyed in the Sunday morning classroom, Christian faith is given every good opportunity to grow strong. This point is particularly made in chapters 3 and 6 through 9, and chapters 6 through 9 offer specific ready-to-use plans for several Bible stories.

But many Sunday school teachers fear using the Bible. So to help with this task, the "good news method of telling Bible stories" is presented in Part II of *CEME*. This approach to the Bible meets with good reports from all over, as the Reverend Donald Seils from St. Paul's Episcopal Church in Leavenworth, Kansas, writes.

> The most exciting application [of the good news method] came for us at our Senior high camp last week, and I'd like to share it with you. The theme for the [Diocese of Kansas] camp was "Name Me Christian," and the various ways we are "named" formed the basis of the program.
>
> Midway through the camp we introduced the story of Jacob and his subsequent "renaming." The campers were then assigned to seven groups with a task of dramatically telling some aspect of Jacob's story. Well—the first thing we encountered was that *none* of the kids *knew* the story. So we "told" it. Then, using the "good news" method and gospel drama (there were about six of us on staff who knew how!), we helped the kids design their skits. *Every single group* was clamoring to be the first to present! When was the last time you saw that happen? The presentations were marvelously creative and humorous, and best of all, the kids really knew the story. They may just remember it for the rest of their lives.

Bible stories generate enthusiasm and satisfaction when handled in the ways suggested in Part II, and with the thirty-plus minutes most teachers have available on Sunday morning, using one Bible story easily generates enough material for four or more consecutive Sundays.

But here we run into an important problem. Many Sunday school teachers fear using the Bible.

I've come to learn that much of this fear results because Bible study was never experienced as very satisfying and least of all, fun. So instead of learning to enjoy the book of God as a grand story of God's love through the ages, many of us remember only complex words, memorizing lengthy genealogies, or learning abstract admonitions that had little connection with our everyday life. We don't want to visit this on the children we love.

Yet still more of our reluctance is generated by modern Bible scholarship. The plain fact is this: modern Bible scholarship has been both a blessing and a curse to the Sunday school teacher. It is a blessing because it delivered us from an all too literal interpretation of Scripture's witness. It has set us free to enjoy the Bible.

But modern day scholarship is a curse because many of us have been made to feel inadequate by scholars who ought to know better. For example, many clergy are so busy explaining who wrote what in the Bible and who did not, what this "really" means and what that doesn't, and whether an event happened this way or another way, that teachers become fearful that they might be teaching the "wrong" thing without knowing what the right thing is.

Episcopal priest the Reverend John Howe makes just this point.

> [W]e must go beyond [the use of these technical tools]. Who cares whether [authors like] J, E, D or P wrote a particular passage? People are literally dying to know what [the Bible] has to say to them. John Rogers of Trinity Episcopal School wryly comments, "We have discovered a way of studying the Bible in which we learn everything about it except what it says."[3]

Alan Jones, dean of Grace Episcopal Cathedral in San Francisco, says the same thing in a different way.

> Biblical studies until recently have been in the grip of a reductionist historicism. There has been too much emphasis on the date, occasion and "original meaning" of a text with little work done on either its use *liturgically* or *devotionally* [emphases mine] over the centuries . . . The results are disastrous. . . .[4]

The results are disastrous, for even gifted teachers have been made to feel inadequate by these highly technical methods.

The few minutes we have in the Sunday morning classroom need far better tools than those used by academics. Not only do we not have the time to use them, we are not about the task of turning out theological scholars. Rather, we are about the business of introducing God's people to God in a personal and purposeful way, and we need make no apology for this.

Part II of *CEME* addresses Bible study directly and creatively and, in addition, poses several other ways to study about God. For example, you and I well know that God's presence and ministry is just as evident in our lives today as it was in the days of the Bible, so chapter 9, "Learning to Speak of God in Today's World," demonstrates a way and the means to discuss God's action in the here-and-now of life today. This subject proves particularly interesting to adults and teenagers and offers a nice balance to the study of God's presence and ministry in Scripture.

A few Bible stories ought to be a part of every year's program of Christian education. Life is a journey; God is always with us; the Bible shows how; and the world is waiting to hear the story. Illustration 1, on the following page, author unknown to me, makes just this point.

THE BOTTOM LINE. When God's ministry and mighty acts are celebrated in story, worship, and play, Christian faith takes an increasing shape in our lives, and Sunday morning Christian education assumes the shape of mission.

1. Poster picture of the journey and the story

𝔚e are simply asked
  to make gentle
  our bruised world
  to tame its savageness
  to be compassionate of all
  including oneself
  then, with the time left over
  to repeat the ancient tale
  and go the way
  of God's foolish ones.

From the ordination invitation of Peter Byrn, S.J., written upon his graduation from the Jesuit School of Theology, Chicago, Illinois.

Step Three: Selecting Other Topics for Study

Maybe you're concerned about "over using" the Bible, and so you ask, "Are there any other topics to help us learn to love the Lord?"

There are, and Part IV of *CEME* lists a host of ideas and suggestions. For example, you can choose to explore the way we help God take care of God's world or what it means to be a modern day saint (during the All Saints term). You can choose the important task of investigating parish history or probe such things as the meaning of the sacraments of baptism and/or the Lord's Holy Communion. The topics just mentioned particularly lend themselves to study during the All Saints, Epiphany, and Easter/Pentecost terms.

You can also include a blessing of the animals during the Easter/ Pentecost term and make this Sunday afternoon a celebration, not only of our relationship to our beloved pets, but a celebration of the fact that we need to aggressively help God take care of the world's environment.

Moreover, your church might have several community ministries that are highly valued, ministries like the support of a community soup kitchen or food pantry, and each one of them also lends itself to a time of study. Provisions for this kind of exploration are seldom provided in store-bought curricula materials.

Even if you tried, you could never run out of things to explore in the Sunday morning classroom. As you can see, there is an abundance of materials available.

But it is the five terms suggested by *CEME* that make it possible every year to schedule *both* Bible study and these other topics of local interest, and to them we next turn.

Step Four: Manage Nine Months Creatively

New Sunday school teachers are often surprised to find themselves scared to death when standing at the front end of the nine-month school year. "Where will I find enough to teach?" they wonder. And, "What happens after October?"

POINT. If these anxious questions are not successfully resolved, the chances are slim that these folks will ever teach again. And because their fright will likely escalate as the year rolls on, both they and their children will suffer.

To make nine months short, successful Sunday school programs break their school year into manageable parts. These educators have learned that when the year drags on and on and on and on without a break, enthusiasm disappears.

2. A "Map" for the year*

THE ALL SAINTS TERM

EARLY SEPTEMBER:
Parish registration.

MID-SEPTEMBER:
The *Celebration of the Ministry of Teaching:* the installation of the teaching staff.

Exploration centers on what it means to be fully human. Study best concentrates on the lives of dedicated women and men from the past and present. We also begin to discern the shape of God's ministry in our midst, helping his world take care of itself. All saints, all of us.

THE CHRISTMAS TERM

MID-NOVEMBER:
The birth of Jesus approaches. Sights are turned to the promise of light and greatness to come.

LATER NOVEMBER:
Thanksgiving Day.

LATE NOVEMBER:
Foodstuffs, to be distributed by a local food agency, are presented at the offertory on the Sunday immediately after Thanksgiving Day.

Since many family members are home from school this weekend, worship becomes an especially powerful celebration. It is like a homecoming. The legacy of sharing at the time of Thanksgiving goes back far beyond the early settlers and the Indians, and it provides a moment of light to lives darkened by hunger.

THANKSGIVING DAY

CHRISTMAS
TERM BEGINS   CHRIST

ALL SAINTS TERM BEGINS

SEPTEMBER   OCTOBER   NOVEMBER 1   DECEMBER
STARTUP   ALL SAINTS DAY

ADVENT I

OCTOBER:
All the saints pledge time, talents, and money to God's church work. Also, we are reminded that all our life is ministry to God, everywhere we work and play.

EARLY NOVEMBER:
The *All Saints Festival.* Every class is encouraged to make a banner or other visual representation of their study. A parish reception in lieu of church school class follows. The saints of God rejoice in their life together, as well as in God's presence.

EARLY DECEMBER:
The first Sunday in Advent. An Advent wreath appears. Light is coming for the world.

LATE DECEMBER:
The *Chrismon Festival.* Large Christmas trees are decorated with Chrismons (symbols of the Christ) made by the children in their classrooms.

Older children may choose to research the reasons these symbols are important in the life of the Church, and they may share their findings with the younger pupils. Intergenerational learning is rich activity.

A birthday party for Jesus follows in the parish hall.

*Adapted from *Creative Christian Education.*
Chapter 8, p. 91-94.

THE EPIPHANY TERM

EARLY JANUARY:
Light has entered the world, and the Church is formed.

The term's focus is on communion, community, and the life of Jesus.

EARLY JANUARY:
An opening *Epiphany celebration.* Epiphany celebrates the visit of the wise men to Jesus. Just as the wise men brought gifts, so we bring them as well, presenting them at the crèche. They will later be delivered to a local hospital's pediatrics unit, providing light for that world. An evening Feast of Lights is also good worship as its educational best.

THE EASTER/PENTECOST TERM

MID-APRIL:
The term's study centers on Jesus' resurrection appearances. Paul's life and ministry become useful vehicles as we take a close look at Jesus through his eyes.

LATE MAY:
An *Ascension Day* theme. Jesus ascends, and we are left with special responsibilities for God's creation. Flowers and other green things may be planted in the *Rogation Sunday* tradition. A *Service for the Blessing of Animals* can be held on a Sunday afternoon.

EARLY JUNE:
The *Pentecost Festival.* God's Spirit empowers Christians for life, and now we begin to return to the seasonal theme of the All Saints term.

Graduation Day for everyone. We take a three-month break because we need it, a "pause that refreshes."

EPIPHANY TERM		LENTEN TERM		EASTER/PENTECOST	
JANUARY	FEBRUARY	MARCH	APRIL	MAY	JUNE

THE LENTEN TERM

EARLY MARCH:
Ash Wednesday

EARLY MARCH:
Studies concentrate on what it is to be "alive to God" in God's world. Jesus is our model, and his quality of life is the quality of life to which we are called. In Easter's shadow we explore the risking quality in Jesus' life, and we dare to explore death, too.

MID-APRIL:
The *Palm Sunday* Festival. Palm branches overhang a grand procession, and the Passion Gospel may end the eucharist as the last gospel reading.

MID-APRIL:
Maundy Thursday. In this evening service the altar and the church are stripped of color and ornament, and the candles are extinguished. Everything is darkened. Worship follows the Palm Sunday experience, fusing the ancient office of Tenebrae with the "Last Supper." This is powerfully visual worship.

MID-APRIL:
Easter Eve. The celebration of God's light for the world.

MID-APRIL:
The *Easter Sunday* Eucharist. The "dead" altar is dressed with color and candles, a cross may be flowered, and worship is the grandest of the year.

LATE FEBRUARY:
"See and Believe" Sunday. Having seen the light of God's Christ, some of the world believes. The story of the Transfiguration is our theme, and on this Sunday before Lent we may also celebrate with baptism, confirmation, and the eucharist. The world responds to the light of the world by saying the "I will" of baptism. This might be a first communion for infant-baptized children.

The celebration concludes with the *Shrove Tuesday* Pancake Supper.

I'm wedded to the use of five terms, each running about six weeks in length, and parts II, III, and IV of *CEME* are particularly focused to help you make your plans using these five terms. The idea for such terms isn't really new. It has been around the church for many centuries, and I'm surprised we haven't used it more.

For example, Advent/Christmas and Ash Wednesday/Lent/Easter are universally recognized as the two most important seasons of the church year, and most Christian education programs recognize them.

CEME makes six-week terms of both these seasons and builds on these two by adding three others. Beginning in September with the

—All Saints term (six to eight weeks), the nine-month school year continues with a

—Christmas term (seven weeks), adds a term to cover the

—Epiphany season (five to eight weeks), includes a

—Lenten term (six weeks), and ends the nine-month school year with an

—Easter/Pentecost term of study (six-plus weeks).

Illustration 2, visualizes this nine-month journey. But more, so that each new period of study can begin afresh, every term must come to a clearly marked close. What I've come to call *show-and-tell worship* makes this possible, and these festivals provide a dramatic pause in the educational journey. They also insure its success by providing an opportunity to display what's been going on in the classroom, and by doing so they offer closure to "what was" so that the parish can happily move toward "what's next?"

POINT. Sunday morning Christian education can't drag on and on and on, no matter how well teachers are equipped to teach. The year-long educational journey needs to be carefully paced, and term-ending festivals meet this need head on with a sensible response.

But I don't mean to leave you with the impression that these festivals are just for the Sunday school community. They are not. They are meant to be a celebration of the previous term of study by the *whole parish at the main Sunday service.*

POINT. When classroom Christian education is brought into the bright light of a jubilee, children feel blessed and special, parents feel blessed and special, teachers feel blessed and special, and everyone else in the parish feels blessed and special. Christian education flourishes in this kind of atmosphere, and as an added bonus you will have no difficulty filling the ranks of teachers year after year.

I've come to expect "standing room only" on these occasions. A party in the parish hall is the perfect conclusion, for it allows everyone to enjoy one another more personally. Making plans for these festivals is discussed in chapter 10 of *CEME,* and chapter 5 shows both the importance and the ways and means to break the nine-month year into manageable parts.

Step Five: Set One Goal and a Few Objectives for the Year

A goal for the year and a few objectives go a long way to insure success in Sunday morning Christian education, and satisfying Sunday morning programs have learned to set both. For example,

> I often ask participants at Christian education workshops how many Bible stories their parish learned last year. It would not be too much to say that many mouths fall wide open, and then puzzled and still later incredulous looks remind me that we leave too much Christian education to chance.
> In fact, most folks cannot briefly tell me what they did in their last year's program. With such an approach, is it any wonder that often we struggle with the purpose or program of Sunday morning Christian education?

Wouldn't it make the task of Christian education easier if, before the year began, you defined a simple-to-understand goal for yourselves and set before your parish a few reasonable objectives? We will look more closely at setting a goal and a few objectives in chapter 12.

But

WHAT IF

> your Christian education program designated four or five stories for congregational exploration during the nine-month year and a decision was made to memorize a few verses of Scripture and to learn to sing a couple of hymns related to these stories?

With these few objectives in mind you would have every good reason to expect the parish to feel like the task of Christian education was far more purposeful than it often appears, and you'd have some objectives whose accomplishment could be readily evaluated at year's end.[5]

Store-bought curricula materials rarely provide for the development of either a parish goal or parish learning objectives, and as a result, sacrificed in your use of these materials is long term vision and parish ownership of the Sunday morning program. Without these two items any Sunday school program is likely to limp at best and fail at worst. The way I figure it, limping is also failing.

A good working Sunday school is built around a sensible program known to every one of the participants, and Part III of *CEME* shows the ways and means of formulating a goal and setting a few objectives for your parish.

Step Six: Don't Use the Public School as a Model for Education

Christian educators know that we can't complete in thirty-plus minutes on Sunday morning what public schools accomplish in six hours every day or thirty hours every week!

We have all too easily linked secular education's formal instruction, with its emphasis on textbook learning, to Sunday School Christian education. The American school model works well to mass produce a literate citizenry in a short amount of time, but it is not a good model for the Christian education.

The public school model too often disables us in the following ways. *First*, there's the matter of quantity. Because the more we learned as school-age students, the better we made our grade, many of us bring the same quantitative expectation to the Sunday school classroom, forgetting that we have only thirty-plus quality minutes with which to work, once a week!

Second, because Sunday School is little different from five-day-a-week school, student boredom and resentment increases. In reaction, teachers, wanting to be faithful and successful, tend to push even more information. And what results? Student acting-out accelerates, and teachers end up feeling guilty as classroom attendance drops off. I've heard more than a few war stories from these burned-out teachers. They often feel like they've let down the parish, their children, and maybe even God. It doesn't have to be this way.

Third, the public school model isn't able to use intergenerational, or interage education. Students are graded according to ages. As a result, many churches, though they call themselves a family of Christians, rarely make use of and therefore can't benefit from interage activities. Chapters 2 and 7 in *CEME* show how this can be much improved.

Fourth, we also learned during our school-age days that an educated and knowledgeable teacher stands at the front of the class dispensing wisdom and information to students who haven't the vaguest idea about the subject. This fact is probably the fundamental reason why it's so difficult to enlist the help of Sunday morning teachers: potential teachers fear they don't know "enough," particularly when Bible study is considered.

What we need to do is put the public school model in its place, the public school, and use its teaching methods as appropriate on Sunday morning. The fact is, "less is more" in the Sunday school classroom, a point made over and over in this book, and a concept that can't "fly well" in the public school classroom.

Sunday school goes best when we have fun exploring a few Bible stories chosen afresh every year, and defining a goal and setting a few realistic objectives makes this happen.

Step Seven: Beware the Danger of Using Store-Bought Curricula Materials

Store-bought materials may seem to offer a good bargain, but they are more costly than they first appear. Here's why. Because they are so complete, and because many Sunday school teachers feel so inadequate, ready-to-use materials discourage teacher creativity and encourage us to refrain from defining a goal. As a result, we teachers often lose the overall vision of what should be happening and how our classroom fits into the whole. We lose the vision of the forest because we are so busy concentrating on one tree, our classroom.

Nor do store-bought materials often relate one class to another, seldom do they include focused periods of study (and the importance of a nine-month "pace" can be denied), and rarely do they provide for show-and-tell worship. Without laboring the point, one can say that store-bought materials often rob a Sunday school of the enthusiasm that only planning together can generate.

Even though most every congregation makes *some* use of store-bought curricula materials, successful Sunday morning programs make every effort to adapt or "customize" these materials to the needs of their church. They do not simply "implant" them, no matter how tempting this might be.

THE BOTTOM LINE. When teachers and parents work together to plan the nine-month school year, when Bible stories are used as a major component, when a goal is defined and few objectives set, and when the nine-month school year is broken into manageable sections, then Christian education is easy and fun, parish fellowship grows by leaps and bounds, and Sunday morning Christian education is a joy, not a task to be finished.

Chapter 2 in *CEME* presents a picture that describes what a built-from-scratch Sunday morning program looks like.

EPISCOPALIA: CUSTOM DESIGN YOUR OWN SUNDAY MORNING PROGRAM

It must be noted that the Episcopal Church has no nationally sponsored Sunday morning program of Christian education, and the 1988 General Convention of the Episcopal Church once again chose not to pursue the development of a denominational curriculum.

In fact, one clergy delegate at that convention reportedly stated that he saw at least six different sets of private vendor curricula materials displayed at the convention site and wondered why the Episcopal Church would ever consider developing more. Now this delegate could be a well-intentioned member of clergy who was in that moment concerned about budgetary constraints. Or even this: he may have been keenly interested in and taken by the wealth of materials present. Or he may simply have been one of those clergy in the Episcopal Church who simply don't care much about what goes on in the Sunday morning classroom, or who every Sunday give thanks that the education burden in their parish is mightily shouldered by those faithful Sunday school teachers who, year after year, are always present.

But in fact, year after year a wealth of materials and a lack of guidance generates this question for those who teach; "What materials should I use?" And there are few guidelines around to offer much help. Indeed, this is one of the reasons Christian education suffers so much in the Episcopal Church, and why Sunday school teachers often feel so much alone.

So which of these store-bought programs should be chosen, and how can *CEME* help with the choice? If you are committed to the use of ready-made materials, *CEME* will encourage you

1. to look for programs that break the nine-month school year into manageable sections. As a result, teachers and students will be defended against the bleak feeling that the year seems to run on and on and on.

2. to look for programs that make provision for occasional show-and-tell festivals, and programs that include the occasional exploration of Bible stories.

3. to evaluate these programs from the perspective of mission. And finally,

4. *CEME* will encourage you to define a goal for the year and help you set a few realistic objectives. As a result, everyone in the parish will know what the future holds, and instead of anxious wonder, both anticipation and satisfaction will reign.

POINT. Using the principles developed in *CEME*, the work of customizing store-bought materials will bring everybody on board in a way never encouraged by simply implanting store-bought materials without attention to development.

Moreover, good help with the presentation of Bible stories is already available in the *Living the Good News* curriculum materials (commonly called the "Colorado Curriculum"). Several years ago the people of the Episcopal Diocese of Colorado began to publish Sunday school materials based on the readings designated by the three-year Prayer Book eucharistic lectionary. This curriculum is now used, say the editors, by better than one-half of the Episcopal church. From what I see, I think their figures are accurate.[6]

But unfortunately, just as other already-prepared curriculum materials can be abused by use straight off the shelf, so can the "Colorado Curriculum," particularly if their ready-made plans are simply implanted on teachers and their students.

This is a better way to use the Colorado Curriculum. Simply
—organize your nine-month teaching year by using the five church-year based terms proposed by *CEME* (this will "pace" your journey and automatically give you periods of short term focus, something the Colorado Curriculum lacks),
—define a goal and think about a few objectives you want to accomplish,
—pick a few Bible stories to use during the year (remembering that less is more),
—choose from *Living the Good News* those materials which offer teaching plans for the Bible stories you have selected,
—add a few other interesting themes and items from Part IV in *CEME*,
—consider the inclusion of a few intergenerational days (see chapter 7 in *CEME*), and finally,
—plan and celebrate your classroom studies by constructing term ending show-and-tell festivals.

Many churches report good results when these two approaches are combined, and I suspect you will find it so as well.

HELP FOR THE TEACHER: MOVING ON TO MAKE IMMEDIATE PLANS

"So," you say, "without revamping our whole program, where is the best place to begin to work in some of the ideas in *CEME*?" I, for one, hope you'll make any revisions in your program with the great care your children and your parish deserve. But here are six ideas that you can begin to implement immediately.

If your present program is running well, I'd plan a show-and-tell festival to celebrate what you're now doing in the classroom. And on the day of the festival I'd have a party in the parish hall for everyone. Festivals capture the atmosphere *CEME* generates, and such a time of worship would give you a good idea about how receptive your congregation would be to the ideas in this book. Chapter 10 is designed to help you make plans for show-and-tell festivals.

Second, if your present program is generating some puzzling questions you can't resolve, chapter 11 offers a trouble-shooting work sheet designed to help you think about these problems in relation to the size of your church.

Third, maybe a class would be interested in constructing a Bible story play for Sunday morning presentation. Several ideas for Sunday morning drama are offered in chapter 6, some involving the whole congregation.

Fourth, I'd think about constructing a day of intergenerational education for everyone in your parish, and chapter 7 offers all sorts of ideas.

Fifth, if you haven't done so already, I'd determine your present goal and begin to think about aggressively supporting the objectives you have already set for yourselves. If a goal and objectives are for the most part unknown to your congregation, tell your people about them. The more a parish knows the reasoning behind your educational program, the more likely your program will sail in smooth winds. Chapter 12 will offer you help with this activity.

Sixth, I'd begin right now to think about planning for next year, and forming a team of interested persons to help me with this task would be an immediate priority.

The rest of *CEME* is designed to help you make plans using the concepts introduced in this first chapter. You will learn to identify and value a mission perspective in Christian education, you will be encouraged to make the Bible your primary teaching resource, and you will be introduced to the ways and means of setting a few realistic objectives easily achieved over the course of a well managed nine-month school year.

By now I hope you can see some of the grand possibilities and promise inherent in creating your own Sunday morning program maybe even from scratch. It does take more work, but there's no better method for success in any endeavor than adding old-fashioned elbow grease to realistic dreams. And what's more, when Christian folks involve themselves in tasks like developing Sunday morning Christian education, God supplies a healthy dose of the support God loves to give and we so much need. In fact, all things begin to work together for good.

Notes

1. Every year I conduct and participate in Christian education workshops around the country. I have researched diverse Christian education programs in such places as McAllen, Texas; Breckenridge, Colorado; Dubois, Wyoming; Virginia Beach, Virginia; Montclair, New Jersey; Baton Rouge, Louisiana; Topeka, Kansas; Asheville, North Carolina, and near my home in northern Virginia, to name just a few locations. I've discovered that parishes excited about Christian education (indeed, enthusiastic about their ministry and growth, which is always closely connected with a satisfying program of Christian education) have learned to recognize the strengths and limitations generated by the size of their congregation. They have a clear goal and some objectives for Christian education. They have settled on a way to organize their parish for the nine-month classroom journey, and they make it a point to celebrate classroom accomplishments. This book is based in part on that research.

2. Carol Phipps, Episcopal Diocese of West Texas, San Antonio.

3. John Howe, "The Irrelevance of Theological Education," *The Episcopalian* 153(February 1988):11.

4. Alan Jones, "Are We Lovers Anymore?" *Theological Education* 24(Autumn 1987):11. The Association of Theological Schools, P.O. Box 130, Vandalia, OH 45377.

5. The place and importance of memorization is discussed in chapter 5 of Howard Hanchey's, *Creative Christian Education*, (Wilton, CT: Morehouse-Barlow, 1986).

6. Enhancing the *Living the Good News* curriculum is discussed more fully in chapter 2 of *CEME*, and their address can be found in that chapter's end notes. See also chapter 5 of *Creative Christian Education* for additional information about using the *Living the Good News* curriculum.

Building a Small Church Sunday School from Scratch

By now I hope you are excited about the prospect of creating your own Sunday morning program, whether from scratch or by "customizing" a store-bought program as *CEME* suggests. The fact is this: simply implementing ready-made materials without attention to making them your own never builds the kind of enthusiasm that marks strong Sunday school programs.

This chapter builds on the discussion begun in chapter 1 and shows that by developing a goal for your Christian education program (what you want to happen); setting a few objectives to help that happen; designating a term or several terms of study; and using several Bible stories, hymns, prayer, occasional memory work, gospel drama, and a few craft projects to provide the content these terms require; it's easy to organize a small church program of Christian education.

But if you are a member of a large congregation, don't make the mistake of thinking this chapter has nothing to offer you, for in it you will see a broad-stroke picture of what a nine-month organizational plan looks like, the way in which only one Bible story will carry forward for several weeks, and you might find your interest stirred by the possibility of intergenerational (or interage) activities.

HOPE IN THE PLACE OF DESPAIR

"But we're too small to have a Sunday school," one announces, while others say, "When we get larger. . . ," and their voices trail off into plans for a future that may never come. Small church despair with Christian education seems rooted in two places.

For one thing, small churches are easily disappointed because they are not large enough to have graded classrooms like those modeled by the public school and the large church. But perhaps even more, because public school education doesn't use the intergenerational model, folks in small churches don't know the power or value of this model. The intergenerational model of education involves people of all ages in the same learning activities, and over and over again it proves a solution to the "problem" of smallness.

MEETING THE CHALLENGE

Suppose you are a member of a small church that has no Sunday school, and suppose you want to begin one. Imagine that you have no more than five children with whom to work, ages three to seventeen years. Suppose also that you have another parent or two who might be interested in helping. Here's what to do.

First, acknowledge that the public school model of graded classrooms will not work for you, for you simply do not have the numbers to support such a model. But since many of us grew up with this model and know it best of all, I would know that potential participants in my hoped-for Sunday school probably think of education only in public school terms. I would be alert to changing this perspective, and I'd make use of the following points.

Large churches generally build their Sunday schools around the public school model of graded classrooms, because graded classrooms make it easy to keep things organized and to deliver information in packages designed for discreet age groups. As a result, small churches often suffer feelings of inferiority when they compare their size and resources with larger congregations.

With only a few minutes normally available to the teacher on Sunday morning (in both large and small churches), what we need to do is this: Have fun with a few Bible stories and make use of crafts, drama, and camaraderie to help the story show God's love and help your students experience God's love in the moment of classroom activity.

Second, I would begin to think about utilizing intergenerational (or interage) education. Intergenerational education takes shape when age groups are combined, and best of all, intergenerational education permits parents to work with both teenagers and smaller children. The last section in this chapter shows intergenerational education at work in a small parish.

The interage model is one that large churches can't often use because of their size. Still, on occasion even the largest of churches can enjoy the opportunities this model generates by developing special craft and activity days designed to bring the entire Sunday school together.

THE BOTTOM LINE. Graded classrooms are good for the large church, but they are not often helpful in the small church setting.

Third, I would offer my interest to my pastor or rector and, if there were support, this is what I would do next. I would set up a meeting with other interested parents or adult parishioners. The telephone would help me get this meeting together.

Fourth, to prepare for this meeting and to present some ideas for the sake of discussion, I'd take a look at the five terms suggested in *Creative Christian Education* (and discussed in chapters 1 and 5 of *CEME*, as well as Part IV). These seasonal terms would give me a place to begin thinking about concrete ideas and lesson plans.

Next I would go to the lectionary we are using in our worship on Sunday morning and pick one Bible story (not a lesson) that fit the term's theme. Because we don't have a lot of time on Sunday morning, I would be guided by the notion that "less is more." It is much better to "milk" one Bible story of all it has to offer than to crowd Sunday morning Christian education with too many lessons.

NOTE. Because the five seasonal terms correlate with most worship lectionaries, you can use any lectionary curricula materials as ready-made resources in your planning. The "Colorado Curriculum," particularly, can be nicely enhanced when the themes of these terms are used.[1]

With this background in mind, in this first meeting I would like to accomplish three objectives with my newly found colleagues.

1. I would want to show how the public school and large church model can't support what we want to accomplish on Sunday morning.

2. I would be prepared to help my new group of colleagues formulate a goal for our about-to-begin Sunday school by discussing

what we want to have happen. The goal might read something like this: "Have fun learning about God by using the Bible." A single, fundamental goal toward which to work is essential when constructing a successful program of Christian education. A goal does not take long to construct, and what it does best of all is set before the parish a vision for the year.

To help this discussion of a goal develop, I'd explore old memories of Sunday school and tease out personal hopes for today by using the "Setting One Goal and a Few Objectives: A Four-Step Plan" (illustration 14) in *CEME*.

3. Finally, I would ask this group to choose for study just one of several Bible stories I had already picked from the lectionary.

Fifth, with this small committee I would begin to consider some of the ways and means suggested in *CEME* to investigate the story and particularly discuss the possibility of developing a play about it. To help this discussion I would be prepared to present some of the ideas discussed in the chapters presenting the good news method of telling Bible stories and gospel drama, chapters 6 through 8. Everyone loves a pageant. Would we use costumes, will there be sets, or could we make a BIG AND BRIGHT banner to picture it? See the fun this generates pictured in illustration 3.

3. All God's Children: Gathering to Worship

(by Gretchen Wolff Pritchard)

MAKE EDUCATION INTERGENERATIONAL

Sixth, I would by now pause to contact the children and their parents, asking them to join me at church on Sunday morning. I would also call other adults who might be interested in participating, and I would treat teenagers as adults.

POINT. Interage education in small churches does not leave out adults who have no small children "to contribute." These educators know that the church itself is a family, and we need to help one another in the task of passing on the tradition.

Seventh, with my now surefooted committee, I'd briefly sketch the details to make our program work. Right from the beginning we would work at making the story into a play, using the "making easy plans to tell a Bible Story" work sheet in chapter 6, and by the time the play is completed participants will know the story from the inside out. See how easy it is?

I would also try to get permission at this early date to present the play to the parish during a future Sunday morning worship service. Everyone likes to express what they learn and later show it to the world. This is where many Sunday school programs go wrong; all the good stuff is locked up in the classroom, and the parish never gets to see it.

Maybe a hymn could be used in the middle of the play, and the whole congregation could join in. Maybe there could be a few special decorations in church on the day of presentation, maybe even a banner or two.

> Now in this play I wouldn't have a lot of lines, but I might make costumes, have fun building some sets, and stress dramatic movement.

> POINT. Learning about God's love takes place easily and naturally around tasks like these, and involving us in and helping us think about God's love for us is precisely what Bible stories do best. The next chapter describes this more fully.

> Teens could help the smaller children, and I'd also feel free to enlist help from other members of the congregation. Intergenerational education begins to take shape.

> With craft tasks like banners and costumes and plays, and still later presentations to others, one Bible story will probably carry through for the whole six weeks.

> POINT. God uses times like these to bind all of us more closely

to himself, and that's what all of us hope for in any effort of Christian education.

CELEBRATE WITH A PARTY FOR THE PARISH

Eighth, after the presentation of the play in church, I'd have a small party for everyone, congregation and fledgling Sunday school.

Ninth, at a later time we might present the play to a local nursing home, a parish shut-in (see *Creative Christian Education,* p. 105), or to the pediatrics unit in the local hospital (see *Creative Christian Education,* p. 129). Of course, we would include the banners and the costumes we had made.

Tenth, after this first event was over we would probably begin the journey all over again, mainly because we had such fun.

VALUE OCCASIONAL CHRISTIAN EDUCATION

If you are a small church and you're not yet ready to begin a full nine-month program, do just a little bit of Christian education at a time and enjoy what you're doing. Don't for a moment think you have to plan a perfect nine-month Sunday school program right from the beginning.

Christian education offered every so often is a perfect approach when it is needed, and as you and your people begin to have fun on Sunday morning, new plans will naturally take shape. Before you know it you'll have a Sunday school program in place that makes sense to you.

Here's how to proceed with occasional Christian education. Designate two or three six-week-long periods during the year and focus your small parish's attention on a Bible story. Tell this story in several different ways, make a play about it and a banner or two, and when all these preparations are complete, present what you've done to the parish.

If this style of teaching is new to you and you want more help, don't miss an opportunity to subscribe to *The Sunday Paper* and *Seedlings. Seedlings,* particularly, offers weekly helps to small church Sunday schools. Addresses are found in this chapter's end notes.[2]

POINT. It is far better to do a little bit of education every once in a while, do it well and have lots of fun, than it is to grind out a "perfect" program, doing things the way they "ought" to be done or "should" be done, and destroy the enthusiasm that inevitably generates when a new Christian education program begins.

DAYS OF INTERGENERATIONAL CELEBRATION: THE MORE THE MERRIER

If you are not yet ready to begin a full nine-month program, you might also be interested in occasional intergenerational days of celebration. These days are, of course, appropriately included in any nine-month program, but if you are not yet at that point in your planning, these days can also stand alone as occasional episodes. Please see chapter 7 for an expansion of this idea.

A *Making a Banner Sunday* can involve your whole parish in the task of picturing a Bible story during a chosen season, or groups of people can be designated to create banners of their own design. Just have plenty of scissors, glue, and banner material handy, along with coffee, juice, and a few pastries. Christmas can be celebrated with a *Making Chrismons Sunday* or a *Making Advent Wreaths Sunday*. The Epiphany season lends itself to a *Making Good News Pictures of Jesus*, or *Making Good News Banners about Our Parish*. And Lent provides an excellent time to prepare for Easter with a *Making Easter Eggs and Butterflies Sunday*.

POINT. If you decide to make a banner, remember that BIG IS BETTER. Less is more when you consider the amount of material to explore over the course of a six-week term of study, but BIG IS BETTER when making a banner.

GOSPEL DRAMA AT WORK IN THE SMALL CHURCH

Here's what one teacher writes about telling Bible stories in her small parish:

> We are a small country church, and because we don't have many children we do a lot of intergenerational education.
>
> Since we hold our Sunday school before we go into church for worship, we sometimes total as many as twenty people (children, ages four to seventeen, and adults) at work on a story project. The numbers change from Sunday to Sunday, of course, but when we use gospel drama, attendance tends to reach a zenith. We also make it a point to have juice, coffee, and a pastry to munch before, during, and after Sunday school.
>
> During the Epiphany term we chose to study the story of the four friends who brought their paralyzed companion to Jesus for healing.

Because the story appeared in the worship lectionary, we thought that if things went well enough we could present it to the congregation when we finished.

Since we were working with a group of children and adults, we planned (beforehand) the following tasks to help us discuss the story: We would

—construct a play, using the good news method of telling Bible stories, (see chapters 6 and 8 in *CEME*),

—take a brief look at God's action in the story and in our lives today (using the work sheet "making easy plans to tell a Bible story"),

—build a banner,

—make simple costumes, and

—construct a simple set. A few parishioners consented to build a set that could be easily and quickly moved into the church.

But like everything else we've ever done using this approach to Christian education, new ideas kept generating. We never did get around to making the banner, but we already have a lovely collection in the parish house which we use in all our festival processions.

This is the story we used, and the characters in the play are italicized.

And when *Jesus* returned to Capernaum after some days, it was reported that he was at home. And *many* were gathered together, so that there was no longer room for them, not even about the door; and he was preaching the word to them.

And they came, bringing to him a *paralytic* carried by *four* men. And when they could not get near him because of the *crowd*, they removed the roof above him; and when they had made an opening, they let down the pallet on which the paralytic lay.

And when Jesus saw their faith, he said to the paralytic, "My son, your sins are forgiven." Now some of the *scribes* were sitting there, questioning in their hearts, "Why does this man speak (blasphemy)! . . . Who can forgive sins but God alone?" And immediately Jesus, perceiving in his spirit that they thus questioned within themselves, said to them, "Why do you question thus in your hearts? Which is easier, to say to the paralytic, 'Your sins are forgiven,' or to say, 'Rise, take up your pallet and walk'? But that you may know that the Son of man has authority on earth to forgive sins"—he said to the *paralytic*—"I say to you, rise, take up your pallet and go home." And he rose, and immediately took up the pallet and went out before them all; so that they were all amazed and glorified God, saying, "We never saw anything like this!"(Mark 2: 1-12, RSV)

We did not develop this story as a miracle event designed to generate awe in the congregation, which of course it does. What we wanted to do was involve both children and adults in an experience of God's action in the Bible and, as we made plans and put the play together, help God touch our hearts with his presence today. Really, isn't that the whole point of studying Bible stories?

Here's the way we worked with the story to develop the play.

1. First we read the story and asked everyone present briefly to share some ideas about what it was like that day. Was it sunny and hot, or was

it rainy? Why was Jesus in the house and not outside like he often was?

2. Then we looked at God's action in the story.

3. Next we divided the story into several scenes (author's note: see the section on scene plays in chapter 6). With only a few children and adults we might include the same participants in every scene.

4. Then we assigned parts to the children and adults. We gave everyone an opportunity to pick the parts they wanted, and some we assigned.

We included only six people to represent the crowd, figuring that if we got the play as far as Sunday worship, the congregation could be the crowd. We also designated four people to be the scribes. As you can see, it doesn't take long to involve a lot of people (which also generates a great discussion).

5. We finally presented the play in church, and because its presentation could have been very complex, to keep it simple, we asked our minister to introduce it and tell the congregation what to look for. We used two narrators to read the lines.

Doesn't her description sound like fun? Chapter 6 of *CEME* describes the scene play that she used as well as several other methods. But make no mistake, the play itself isn't the most important event in this method of Bible study. What is most important is the discussion that goes into developing the play.

Christian education is easy in the small church setting. But it means using some tools that were never shown to most of us as we grew to adulthood, and it means getting rid of a few all too familiar and disabling ideas.

Notes

1. The popularly named "Colorado Curriculum" is more correctly identified as the *Living the Good News* curriculum. Enhancing this curriculum is discussed ever more explicitly in chapter 5 of *Creative Christian Education*, pg. 45.

2. If you need help with drama, pageants, and related activities, *The Sunday Paper* offers superb help with drama and other learning activities. It is written and published by Gretchen Wolff Pritchard, 19 Colony Road, New Haven, CT 06551.

Seedlings provides ready-to-use Sunday morning lesson plans coordinated with the eucharistic lectionary, and it also meets with an enthusiastic welcome in many places. Write *Seedlings*, Box 1062, San Marcos, TX 78667.

CHAPTER THREE

Helping God Make Believers of Christians

This chapter is written for teachers, parents, and clergy who want to know more about God's action in the Sunday morning classroom. "What can we expect of God's ministry in the enterprise of Christian education, and what difference does God's presence make in the Sunday morning classroom?" Questions like these burn hot for mission-minded teachers, and this chapter discusses both of these concerns.

POINT. Christian education is fundamentally God's ministry, not our own. Let there be no mistake, we teachers play an important part. But when we know the shape of God's ministry in the lives of God's children, both young and old, those of us called to teach feel much better about our task, and rarely feel very much alone anymore.

In particular, the following pages will help you understand the way in which God engages both small children, teenagers and adults, and as a result you will find the teaching strategies that best help you and your charges meet and be met by God.

Use a pencil to mark the ideas that excite your interest. In the first half of this chapter I'll show you how to value your participation in God's ministry of Christian faith's birth and growth (and isn't this our most important task?), and in the second half I'll show you the way God uses Holy Communion as a powerful educational event and why, until the last several years, most of the Christian church in the Western world stopped using it as such.

As a result of your readings in this chapter, I believe you will more clearly understand the way you can help the Sunday morning educational ministry of the One whom we love so much. Also, you should come to a position of more confidently valuing the "playful" activities that I like to include in the Sunday morning classroom, activities that have in the past been too much discounted by educators compulsively driven by the public school model of education.

WHEN DID THE SUNDAY SCHOOL BEGIN?

Many Sunday school teachers are greatly helped by just a brief discussion about the origins of Sunday morning Christian education.

For those interested in a little-known but important historical fact, note this point: The first Sunday school was not founded by Robert Raikes in Gloucester, England, in 1780, as it is commonly believed (see *Creative Christian Education*, page 157 for more about Mr. Raikes). In fact, Christian education began as soon as the first infant child was baptized, and that was sometime in the first century. Right from that moment parents, sponsors, congregation, and clergy began to think about making believers of those just-baptized infants, and I dare say that the first Sunday school teacher was recruited at about this same moment.

We who teach today follow in this grand tradition and, almost twenty centuries later, we are still about the task of helping God make believers of infant baptized children.

THE BOTTOM LINE. Sunday morning Christian education has evolved to this point in the American west: It values the entire Sunday morning experience, from getting ready at home (with family enthusiasm an important ingredient), to arrival at church and later departure for home, and it combines church fellowship, worship and the classroom into a unity wherein we can meet and be met by God, and we know it. In such a place God is given every opportunity to slowly transform "natural faith" into "Christian faith," to be discussed in just a moment.

Today's arrangement of a Sunday school does not take the shape of the one designed by Robert Raikes, nor does our model follow the pattern of a "Sunday school" in the early church. But given the demands of the twentieth century, the model noted above is the shape of a Sunday school that works for us.

MISSION-MINDED CHRISTIAN EDUCATION

Growing congregations are always strong on Christian education, and each one has determined a style that works well for them. Their approach may look like the one described above, and they devote a lot of energy to this ministry.

Indeed, more than a few congregations even develop "bus ministries" to bring children to church, knowing that where the children are so might follow their parents.

Still, you may be also familiar with popular news reports that suggest, I believe simplistically, that many if not all growing churches are characterized by a fundamentalist approach to Scripture and tradition.

Pollsters like George Gallup fuel this perspective.

> In the last two decades, many middle-class Americans have left mainline churches, with their emphasis on social programs, and joined the evangelical movement, attracted by a more inward-looking faith and clearer, stricter instruction in moral values.
>
> As many as one-third of Americans call themselves evangelical, according to George Gallup Jr., himself an evangelical.[1]

This article goes on to show that in the period 1965 to 1985, the Assemblies of God (formerly the church of Jimmy Swaggart and Jim and Tammy Bakker) grew from about 500,000 to a few more than 2,000,000, while the Southern Baptist Convention expanded from slightly less than 11,000,000 to about 14,500,000.

During this same period of time
— the United Methodist Church lost 2,000,000 members, declining from about 11,000,000;
— the Presbyterian Church (USA) lost 25 percent of its membership, down to 3,000,000 from a high in 1965 of 4,000,000 members; and
— the Episcopal Church declined from about 3,400,000 to 2,900,000 communicants (losing an additional 400,000 members in 1986).

At first glance it seems that pollsters like Gallup are right. But this is the plain fact; there are fundamental churches not growing one whit while more than a few mainline, "liberal" churches are growing dramatically.

POINT. Church growth is not dependent upon how Scripture is approached *but how God's ministry is valued,* and growing churches are marked by the same mission mind-set that characterizes successful Sunday morning Christian education.

For example, in less than twenty years the Church of the Apostles, an Episcopal church in Fairfax County, Virginia, grew from the twelve people who organized it to a congregation with an annual budget well in excess of $1 million. This congregation markedly differs from the Episcopal Church at large, a denomination losing more than 17 percent of its membership since 1980. My point is that the Church of the Apostles is just one of many mainline churches in America growing at a pace that exceeds the expansion of their local community.[2]

But even when mission-minded congregations are located in static communities where possibilities for growth are less evident or even less possible, they are still marked by the same joyous and expectant spirit characterizing those first-century congregations that prevailed. Along with their clergy, each one of these congregations likes nothing better than to talk about God's presence and ministry, whether in the Sunday morning sermon, at coffee hour, in the Sunday school classroom, or at Bible study. Indeed, their enthusiasm fuels the engine that drives their Sunday morning program of Christian education. In this chapter I want you to catch a vision of their vision, and let it inform your plans as you think best.

EXAMINING GOD'S EDUCATIONAL MINISTRY

God is always at work in our midst, and mission-minded Christian educators know that the infant baptized children and adults whom we serve on Sunday morning were made Christian by God at baptism. But none of these infants could at their baptism be called believing Christians. Right off the bat, this is an important distinction to be made. One or two month old infants simply aren't interested in declaring the Apostle's Creed.

Yet marvelously and mysteriously, even these infant baptized persons are people of faith, and although their faith cannot yet be called Christian, the "natural faith" they do possess is generated by God. Moreover, it is also this "natural faith" that provides the cradle for "Christian faith's" later birth and growth.

POINT. The transformation of "natural faith" into "Christian faith" is of keen interest to those of us committed to Sunday morning Christian education. It provides the encouragement and the authority we use to work with notions such as "less is more," and to use the playful activities we have learned to value so much.

Valuing the Gift of our Children's Natural Faith

Above all else Christian education is concerned with the birth and growth of Christian faith. But to understand Christian faith, it is first of all necessary to understand its antecedent, natural faith.

"So what is natural faith?" you ask. It is this: Natural faith is the natural human response to God's presence and ministry in our lives. "Natural faith" is not a belief in God, and it is not dependent upon going to church or hearing about God. Natural faith is solely dependent upon the cosmic breadth of God's amazing grace and God's love for every one of us. Here in a nutshell is the story of the forgiving father and the prodigal son (Luke 15: 11-32) and the good Samaritan (Luke 10:29-37).

Natural faith is born around the world and it is born in every citizen. Because of natural faith we of the world learn to trust even when there are no promises present. Around the world we learn to lean toward love, not hate; we learn to lean toward hope even when life is full of despair and, even when vengeance demands to be heard, we learn to pardon those who wrong us. We learn that where there is darkness we can hope to see signs of light, and that even when there is discord we have reason to work for union.

"Natural faith" is basically an attitude of trust, and it is developed by God around the world long before any of us knows God's name. Infants particularly are children of natural faith, born with a God-inspired trust about the righteousness of God's universe.

Of course, we do not consciously know that this attitude is God-inspired, and we will never know it until we are told of it. That's where the Sunday morning classroom plays a special part in God's ministry of Christian faith's development.

In short, whether young or old, our students come to us as God-touched people known by God even before they were formed in the womb (Jer. 1:4). Theirs is a deeply formed faith rooted in godly trust, even if they do not yet know God by name.

Natural Faith Becoming Christian Faith

Natural faith has nothing whatsoever to do with conscious knowledge of God. It has nothing to do with belief. Because God loves us we learn to trust the world. Because we are loved by God, natural faith is born and grows.

Still more insight on natural faith is offered by two words the Hebrews used to identify it, Amen and Batah. Amen has to do with a sense of solidity and sureness, and Batah suggests an attitude of security and confidence. The New Testament book of Hebrews (11:1) even puts it this way:

> "Faith is the substance of things hoped for, and makes us certain of realities we do not see."

POINT. Natural faith is not a commodity to be given nor a set of facts to be known. Natural faith is the natural human response to God's presence in our lives. What God gives us is God's presence, and the human response is what we call faith, a sort of awareness that there's "more around me and in me than me." So rejoice for the gift of natural faith, for its presence signs God already at work in the lives of your students.

But when God is present and known by God's biblical identity to be present, *Christian faith* takes shape. This is an especially important notion for us to understand.

Natural faith converts to Christian faith when the first bit of Christian knowledge is added to it. But just as the connection of the sperm and egg in the womb do not make a fully developed human being, this nascent interest doesn't make a full-blown Christian person. But the mold is cast, and with a little help from Sunday morning Christian educators, Christian faith begins to grow strong. Illustration 4 makes just this point.

Rarely do we teachers engage children of three years or older on Sunday morning with no sign of Christian faith present in their lives. Even the least of these small ones has heard God named, they may even call "church" the place "where God lives," and they didn't get this information from the daily newspaper. Mission-minded classroom teachers value the task of helping God nurture this budding Christian faith, and moving it along toward the sturdiness that marks maturation.

Natural faith becomes Christian the more we come to know the sovereign God of the universe through events like the study of Bible stories (the reason I so much like Bible study on Sunday morning), Sunday morning worship, experiences with Sunday school teachers, hearing God named, and celebrating God's ministry today. Natural faith becomes distinctly Christian when we learn to know that Jesus is the only perfect image of the Father, and that he shows us the nature of God.[3]

THE BOTTOM LINE. Whenever people in the world begin to believe that another, higher power is the God of Abraham and Sarah, Isaac and Rebecca, Jacob and Rachel, and the God and Father of

4. Making believers of Christians

Coming to Consciously Know God

Life Line: God with us from birth to death

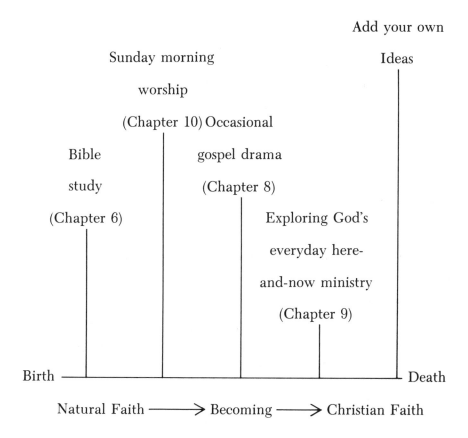

our Lord Jesus Christ, Christian faith begins to take shape. Faith's birth and growth lies within the realm of God's ministry, but we can help, and we help best by creating an environment wherein God is known to be present. Hence, good Sunday morning Christian education helps birth Christian faith by involving students in an exploration of God's action in Bible stories, paying particular attention to the Gospel accounts of Jesus' life and ministry.

Mission-minded teachers cultivate a classroom atmosphere of expectation and enthusiasm, and no better assets are available to help you than arts and crafts activities related to Bible stories. The fact is, when we explore together, laugh together, create together, and celebrate together, God comes especially because our defenses are down. Jesus meant exactly this when he talked about the "little children." *CEME* is written to help you promote this happening.

The "Conversion" of a Saint

The conversion of natural faith to Christian faith is shown in the following story. It happened this way.

I always begin the nine-month teaching year with an All Saints term of study, and that term pays particular attention to the way in which all of us are saints in God's world. To illustrate modern day sainthood, I like to invite firefighters, medical physicians, rescue squad members, and police to the church on Sunday.

For adolescents, these explorations provide an opportunity to explore how they might spend their lives in their adult future. And for adults, explorations can happily center on God's providential care of his world, through us, and the ways in which God has called us to our occupations. When this kind of teaching takes place hearts and minds are sparked by God with new perspectives about the way we and God are joined in a mutual ministry to take care of his world.

One year a firefighter remarked on the occasion of his Sunday visit, "I never thought of myself as a saint." Children clambered over the truck he brought, they handled his gear, and all the while, I later learned, he was just a little embarrassed as they kept referring to him as a saint.

But a year later he was baptized.

This firefighter came to us as a person of natural faith. Because of God's care he had learned to care about the world, and he enjoyed defending it from the ravages of fire.

But he did not come to us as a Christian.

As a result, some Christian purists venture that he should not be considered a saint. But that's to nickel and dime this important point, for even though he might not measure up to the stature of Mother Teresa, in God's eyes he was a saintly son long before he knew he was a child of God.

In fact, this firefighter had never given much thought to God or godly things. "But the kids kept referring to me as a saint, and while I was standing by the truck I heard their teacher explaining how I helped God take care of the world and how God needed my help, and that got me to thinking more and more."

God moves in the world in quiet, caring ways, bringing his folk to new life and new knowledge.

Just as a human pregnancy results when a sperm and egg connect, and just as the product of that connection will differ from the newborn baby and the forty-year-old person, so Christian faith grows over a lifetime. A newborn Christian's faith looks far different after forty years than it looked when he or she was first baptized, but that difference is generated by God. Parents who know this baptize their infant children with joy and know also that the task then before them is that of helping the children continue to grow in the knowledge and love of the Lord, which is precisely the place where we Sunday school teachers play our part.

The more we involve our students in Bible related activities on Sunday morning, the more likely natural faith will give way to Christian faith. With some students, growth will quickly show; with others the process will be slower. But God is always working to help it happen, and God simply asks for a few activities from us to give him the ways and means.

POINT. We are made Christian at baptism, whether we are adults or infant children, but we become believing Christians when natural faith is shaped by the witness of Scripture and the New Testament. Good Sunday morning Christian education never diminishes the importance of natural faith, and always seeks to nurture Christian faith.

If you want children to begin the journey toward Christian faith, put them in places where God is known to be present, like the Sunday morning classroom. One can't guarantee Christian faith's birth; that's an issue lying between God and the child. But we can plant the lives of our children in growth-producing environments like the Christian church, and in that place Christian faith is more likely to develop than not.

The Lifelong Journey of Faith

Rarely do we in the classroom have an opportunity to see the long-term growth and maturation of those whom we teach, be they children, teens, or adults. We work with our charges for a year or two, they move to another town, or we do, or their paths take them one place and ours take us to another. And so we wonder, "Did I make any difference?" "Did I do OK?" "Is it worthwhile?"

The following story presents one person's journey in faith and a picture of her maturation over the years. It is not the story of a classroom event (several such stories, however, are presented in chapters 4 and 6 of *Creative Christian Education*). But you'll plainly see evidences of natural faith and its growth toward Christian faith. And what's more, the same events that made a difference for her are precisely the quality of the events you doubtless work so hard to effect in your classroom teaching.

Jane describes her spiritual journey this way:

> Sunday was a special day in my family. What set it apart was the fact that without fail our family attended Sunday services regularly, during the school year as well as on vacation.
>
> Each summer our family vacationed for three months at our beach cottage on the Atlantic coast of North Carolina. On Sundays we children put on "Sunday clothes" and struggled to get our sunburned feet back into now-tight shoes.
>
> After gathering up all the children in the neighborhood, my father drove our full car across the long bridge to the mainland. There, in a tiny whitewashed church, we'd have an opening time of fellowship singing hymns like, "He Leadeth Me, O Blessed Thought." It was a big gathering, adults and children together. Then we children would be herded off by age groups to Sunday school classes.
>
> When church was over, all of us hopped in the car and headed for the beach. Then came the really big treat of the day. My father always stopped at a grocery store owned by a Mr. Barefoot. The name always struck me as very appropriate for the beach.
>
> And all of us were treated to a popsicle. Here was our after-Sunday-school ritual, standing outside Mr. Barefoot's, by now shoeless again, and me with an orange popsicle dripping all down the front of my Sunday dress in the hot North Carolina sun.
>
> I cannot remember much about what I "learned" in that tiny little whitewashed church. What I do remember is the habit of churchgoing, even during vacation. I still go to church year 'round.
>
> This cumulative childhood experience is one of my greatest legacies from my parents. It put meaning for me into the Fourth Commandment from early on, "Remember the Sabbath day to keep it holy . . . the Lord blessed the Sabbath day and hallowed it."
>
> Somehow, though I didn't know it then, God was also hallowing me, making me a bit more whole as a child of his.[1]

I understand Mr. Barefoot still runs that small store in Duck, North Carolina, on the Outer Banks of that state. But to this day he may be unaware of his participation in God's ministry of binding this woman to himself during a series of years more than four decades ago.

THE BOTTOM LINE. With a little support from parents, children move easily from natural faith to a deeper and more personal faith in God's love and care for them.

Christian Faith in Children, Teens, and Adults: Teaching Strategies

I've learned to make two judgments when considering the ways and means of helping God strengthen Christian faith, and both assist in the development of effective teaching strategies for all age groups.

Because Christian faith takes a different shape in children and adults, I've learned to value both a "feeling component" and a "thought component." Christian faith is a combination of both components, it is not simply one or the other, and good teaching honors both.

The feeling side of Christian faith I call *trustful love,* and this concept is particularly important when considering the faith development of small children. Trustful love in response to God's presence took shape during visits to a beach over the course of several years, and it took a small shape in the life of the Sunday morning visit of a firefighter. You can also count on trustful love taking shape as you and your children have fun exploring Bible stories, or make banners, or create plays.

POINT WHEN TEACHING SMALL CHILDREN. Because the faith of small children tends to be characterized by trustful love, up through grade seven plan your teaching with this notion in mind. Tell Bible stories, act them out, make banners, organize field trips. A bucketful of more suggestions are listed in Part IV of *CEME.*

But as we Christians grow from childhood to adulthood, the more we begin to approach the gospel of God's love with our minds, adding to trustful love both reason and hope. We wonder, "Why do bad things happen in the world if God is so good?" and, "What does God want from me?" We sometimes even ask, "Is there a God, or is this just some sort of fairy tale?" Good teaching honors the adult search to make sense of things, and Part IV of *CEME* offers ideas and suggests topics when working with both teenagers and adults.

POINT WHEN TEACHING TEENS AND ADULTS. Value the continued development of trustful love, but particularly support the growth of faith as reasoned hope. Encourage teenagers and adults to take issue with Scripture's stories of God's action and human life, because when honest questions are asked in a community of faith, God helps us with some answers. The adult search to make sense of things, always wondering why, is an expression of our reaching for reasoned hope.

THE BOTTOM LINE. Younger children respond more to God with their hearts and feelings. The older we grow, the more we also engage God with our thinking processes. Our head and heart walk hand-in-hand, though in matters of faith our hearts tend to travel slightly first.

GOD'S ACTION AT THE TABLE: YOUNG CHILDREN AND THE EUCHARIST

Many "traditionally brought-up" Christians wonder why many modern day churches admit even infants to Holy Communion. "Are we losing all sense of dignity?" some wonder, while others see this as an overly permissive response, even a "watering down" of Christian faith and practice. In fact, what is happening is far richer and more positive than any of these concerns.

The plain fact is this: if you want to bring up children in the Christian faith, don't deny them the fellowship of the Lord's table. The communion rail is God's preeminent classroom. It might not look like a classroom to most of us, but eyes of faith can't see it as anything else. Here's why.

The word *education* is rooted in the latin educare, meaning "to lead forth" or "to bring up." It's as simple as this: God uses the Holy Communion to lead us into a deeper and more personal relationship with him. Here is powerful education, not the book-learning kind but the type God seems to enjoy using best of all.

Those who limit the participation of children until they "understand" the eucharist are on the wrong track. God's Holy Communion is a means of grace; for through it Christian faith is strengthened, and because of it natural faith begins to become Christian.

A story helps make this point.

> A while back I participated with a group of five- and six-year-old children learning about communion. I was a member of their congregation.
>
> I was particularly impressed by the way the presiding priest was able to help shape their enthusiasm and interest, not pushing too much information, but depending upon and using their curiosity as bread and wine were handled. There was a lot more commotion than eleven o'clock Sunday's worship, but it was not at all disrespectful.
>
> What I saw most of all was this. In the hubbub of twisting bodies, questions, and an occasional punch or two as room was made at the rail,

I saw the marketplace of life, and above it all I heard the words, "The body of our Lord Jesus Christ keep you in everlasting life." The children heard it too, perhaps through ears smaller than mine, but amplified by God's presence in their lives.

Natural faith's development was clearly evident in their fellowship and joy, and as well I felt my own faith teased to life.

But are there any signs of the belief that begins to characterize the faith we call Christian? I think so, but the truth of it only later surfaced.

Later the same day, one of these six-year-old students wanted to join his nine-year-old brother at a late afternoon movie. Since Mom and Dad were already committed to something else, they said no, not wanting the boys in the shopping mall all by themselves. But the boys persisted, and finally the youngest—who'd participated in the communion service just that morning, pulled his trump: "But we won't be alone. Jesus will be with us."

Chuckle if you will, but there's a mystery here. Being added to natural faith is knowledge of God. And at precisely this point natural faith is beginning to become Christian faith in this six-year-old child's life.

God is always about the business of touching our lives, and when we begin to talk about God's presence and ministry in places like the Sunday morning classroom, deep within God whispers, "It's true."

Holy Communion and the Growth of Christian Faith

Water baptism is the way we are born into the Christian church family, and once we're born into any family we need to be fed. Just like meals at home provide for spiritual and emotional health, so too communion at the Lord's table generates spiritual strength and births knowledge about who we are and to whom we belong.

In most denominations, only people able to reason as adults are admitted to the Lord's table. Adult baptism is a prerequisite to being fed at the Lord's table, or the rite of confirmation for those persons baptized as infants. And the assumption is this: human instruction and cognitive knowledge are necessary before we approach the Lord's table.

But if family life at home were constructed this way, if we had to know our name and how to spell it, if we had to know such things as family history—and the list goes on and on—none of us would be around to grow up. The fact is, this method of pre-communion education, as well meaning as it is, does not much acknowledge God's teaching ministry in the Holy Communion.

For just a moment think about what it's like to be fed as a Christian. Learning Bible stories is one kind of feeding, and prayer is another way we are nurtured by God. But there's still another way God helps us grow up, though it's often closed to young children. God feeds us in the breaking of the bread, and as the action of communion is interpreted by the words of communion—"This is my body," "This is my blood"—natural faith slowly becomes Christian.

Here is a mystery. And it's a mystery deepened by this surprising fact: though we human beings are always learning, we also learn even before we're born.

The brain is not an organ switched on at birth, nor even a few days or months after birth. We begin the process of learning while we're being formed in the womb. Writer Muriel Beadle offers insight:

> The psychologists Jack Bernard and Lester W. Sontag once tested fetal response to sound by placing a loudspeaker close to the mother's abdomen (but not in contact with it, to assure that sound waves would travel through air).
>
> They found that the broadcast sound caused the rate of fetal heartbeat to increase sharply. This didn't prove, of course, that the unborn baby was hearing—only that it was sensitive to sound stimulus.
>
> Something a little more ambitious was then attempted by David K. Spelt (who, like Jack Bernard and a number of other psychologists mentioned in these pages, started out in academic life but shifted to consultative work for business).
>
> Spelt's experiment was to use sound in "conditioning" unborn babies; that is, he decided that he would try to teach them to transfer to stimulus B a response originally elicited by stimulus A.
>
> Spelt's version of this kind of experiment began by securing the cooperation of sixteen pregnant women who were past the seventh calendar month of gestation.
>
> He divided them into several groups. With one group, he ascertained that a vibrator applied to a maternal abdomen would not disturb the fetus sufficiently to cause movement. Experience with another group showed that a loud noise just outside the mother's body (an oak clapper hitting a pine box) *would* cause fetal movement. Then, using a third group, Spelt combined the vibrator and the sound—timing them so that there was a few seconds' lag after he started the vibrator and before he loosed the clapper.
>
> After 15-20 pairings of the vibrator-plus-sound, the fetuses began to move in response to the vibrator alone. In two cases, the experiment was interrupted for more than two weeks, yet when the expectant mothers returned to Spelt's laboratory, their unborn babies "remembered" the experience and again moved in response to the vibrator alone.
>
> Such experiments are not as bizarre as they might at first seem to a layman.

> Birth is really only one point in developmental time, one event in a continuum of existence—the beginning of which has a special aura of mystery because it is hidden."[5]

It's hard to say when we're ever too young to learn, and harder still to describe God's participation in our learning processes. But this is the fact, we do learn from the very earliest age and God participates. Let's don't get in the way.

Welcome Even the Smallest

How did we get into the present bind of keeping baptized children from the fellowship of the Lord's table? A bit of history helps, and to make the discussion as simple as possible, I'm going to divide it into a brief exploration of four historical periods: A.D. 30 to 400, 400 to 1200, 1200 to 1960, and finally the last thirty years.

First, we must note that as far as we know, no children were baptized in the first century of the Christian church. Baptism was withheld until candidates for membership could be certified as believers, and as far as the first-century church was concerned, only adults were ready to make this kind of affirmation.

But not many years later, as the church grew older and as believing parents wanted to include their children in the Christian fellowship, on the basis of *their promise* to bring up their children in the knowledge and love of the Lord, bishops extended baptism to the infant children of believers. In addition, a rite of confirmation was instituted to "complete" the infants' baptisms when they reached adult years, and at that time they were expected to affirm the promises and vows made for them by their parents.

Because bishops were the chief ministers in those early and small congregations, they were expected to preside at both the eucharist and the event of baptism. And they expected to preside. But then there arose a complication. Toward the end of this first three-hundred-year epoch, the emperor Constantine made the Christian church the official church of the Roman Empire, and church growth dramatically accelerated. Now we come to the second period.

This second historical period spans the years A.D. 400 to 1200. Because spectacular church growth continued, many new congregations were established. But because bishops could not be in more than one place at a time, they delegated the sacrament of baptism (which formerly they alone conducted) to priests. From this time forward, local parish priests, not the bishop, celebrated both Holy Communion *and* baptized. Soon infant baptism grew to be the norm, and as soon as these infant children were baptized, they were admitted to the Lord's table. However, still reserved for the bishop was the rite of confirmation, the adult affirmation of a mature Christian faith.

Church growth did not slow, however. In fact, it continued to escalate, and episcopal visits for confirmation were scheduled more and more infrequently. And here was the rub: fewer and fewer of these infant-baptized Christians presented themselves to the bishop for confirmation. As a result, a growing number of bishops felt that both Christian faith and the life of the church were being seriously compromised. So in the twelfth century, Bishop Peckham decreed that no baptized Christian would be admitted to communion until they had been confirmed. His decree is known to this day as Peckham's Discipline, and for the last eight centuries the Western Christian church has been working under his rule.

Now we are living at the front edge of the fourth period, one I suspect will carry us into the indefinite future. Although the admission of young baptized children to the eucharist is not quite two decades old, the practice itself shows the Western Christian church is beginning to align itself more closely with the second- and third-century church by connecting the baptism and feeding of Christians, just as birth and feeding are connected in family life. Though we lost this vision for eight-hundred years, we are now recovering a thousand-year-old tradition by saying that no baptized person ought be denied feeding once they are born into the Christian family.

What this means for the church is this: gently, over the course of Sundays and through their early years, natural curiosity, the mystery of the eucharist, and God's action at the table combine to form children as Christians. Here is education of profound proportions, the kind that God enjoys best of all.

We more than flirt with "works righteousness," the notion that knowledge or action makes us presentable to God, when we delay first communion until a time of understanding or belief. More, the medium of precommunion preparation much in vogue today too often conveys the message that baptized persons need to "be more" or "know more" in order to find a welcome by God at his table.

This is the plan I like best of all. From the earliest age, young children ought to share the Lord's table with their families of origin, or some other sponsor if a family member isn't available. There they are powerfully engaged by God. Then, as verbal questions take shape, good education provides for rational dialogue. This can take place formally and informally in the Sunday morning classroom and at home as well. Here the participation of parents or other sponsors is a too seldom used asset.

And this is what will happen.

> Childhood curiosity and imagination combine with God's action to generate the nativity of Christian faith.
>
> And why can this conclusion be drawn? I've heard more than one small child say, "Jesus," as the host is offered.

So instead of holding "communion classes" for children so that they might "understand better," involve children in communion from the earliest age, provide God an opportunity to stir their natural curiosity, and then answer their God-inspired questions. Illustration 5 captures a bit of the atmosphere I hope you'll work to create.

For the first time in almost eight hundred years the Western Christian church is beginning to recognize again the power of the table's fellowship and God's use of it. We are moving away from the excesses of rationalism and its worship of knowledge as the first good, a powerfully present force in the church since the eighteenth century. Knowledge and thinking are important for the Christian, but the Western Christian church is learning afresh that experience (from the earliest age) and God's ministry also count in the province of faith development.

Notes

1. Laura Sessions Stepp, "The Evangelical Challenge, Many Americans Leave Mainline Churches," *Washington Post*, August 17, 1987.

2. Figures supplied by the Commission on Evangelism and Renewal, and reported to the 1988 General Convention of the Episcopal Church in the Blue Book, the official publication of reports and resolutions considered by the bishops and deputies at that sixty-ninth General Convention.

3. The Book of Common Prayer describes the emergence of Christian faith this way in the Outline of Faith (p. 849) by answering the question, "What do we mean when we say that Jesus is the only Son of God?" Answer: "We mean that Jesus is the only perfect image of the Father, and shows us the nature of God."

4. From Howard Hanchey, *Creative Christian Education* (Wilton, CT: Morehouse-Barlow, 1986), pg. 30.

5. Muriel Beadle, *A Child's Mind*, (New York: Jason Aronson, 1974), pp. 3-5. Beadle sites several studies on the way human beings learn from times before the birth event. Data like this encourages an appreciation for our early readiness to meet God and respond to God's first overtures.

5. **Children in church. Gretchen Wolff Pritchard, adapted from the cover of the Living Church.**

Celebrating Together with Children

If children are genuinely to participate, the space in the chapel, and the liturgy itself,

must be arranged so they can see, move and do things.

Design by Gretchen Wolff Pritchard. Adapted from the cover of THE LIVING CHURCH, November 13, 1988.

CHAPTER FOUR

Faith Seeks Understanding: Planning Education for Adults and Teens

Most Sunday school programs are quick to pay attention to the education of small children, but are less attentive to the needs of teens and adults. Yet adolescent and adult Christians hunger even more than small children for a discussion of God's love and action in their lives and often long for someone to help this happen. Growing churches have listened to these hungers of the heart, and their programs in response generate all kinds of satisfaction.

This chapter continues the discussion of God's action offered in chapter 3 and offers specific guidelines for work with both teens and adults. Moreover, when joined with the ideas for teaching teens and adults described in Part IV of *CEME*, you will find every good reason to hope for a successful program.

ATTENDING THE NEEDS OF ADULTS AND TEENS

"Why lump teens and adults together in one discussion?" asks a colleague. The fact is this: from the time we turn from the first ten years of our life, "why" questions loom larger and larger. As a result, both adults and teens begin to reason about God and the vagaries of life.

FAITH SEEKS UNDERSTANDING

Adults are always interested in understanding more about their faith, and teenagers are rapidly moving toward this same place.

The concept of faith seeking understanding is a gift from Anselm, a twelfth-century archbishop of Canterbury. As a result of his interest he came to see that all theological inquiry is a combination of personal faith and human questions reaching for understanding.

THE BOTTOM LINE. Sunday morning education for adults and teenagers, whenever it seeks to understand matters of faith, is theological education at its best. And even if their theological questions are not precision tuned, important questions are present that deserve to be answered. Chapters 6 through 9 are particularly designed with the education of adults and teenagers in mind.

MEETING ADULT NEEDS

Adult Christians are always interested in talking about God, not in the abstract, but in ways that help them make sense of everyday life. Adult education on Sunday morning is successful when it challenges what we know and helps us change our perspectives.

Five qualities mark adults who participate in Sunday morning classes, and because these qualities are present, you have every good reason to expect success.

First, you can count on enthusiasm. They are not in your class as convicted criminals. They are present because they have been invited by God and they have been faithful in response. They may not think God had a thing to do with their presence, but that should not prevent you from seeing the obvious and affirming it when appropriate.

Second, adults are interested in self-discovery. They want to find out more about themselves and about who God is. These folks are personally interested in what is being discussed, and only in rare cases are they present because someone forced them.

Third, they want to learn something that they did not know before, and they enjoy the task of acquiring new perspectives.

WARNING. Adults don't want a teacher who, because she or he has not prepared, simply says, "Now, what do you think of this?" after making a brief statement. A question like this is, however, entirely appropriate when an idea has been presented that's designed to foster discussion. But if this question is asked in lieu of ideas that stir interest, you have every reason to expect disappointment from your class.

Fourth, adults like practical perspectives that will make a difference in their lives. For example, developing their capacity to see signs of God's presence and ministry in the here and now of everyday life is just this kind of information. Chapters 8 and 9 in *CEME* offer all kinds of help in this area.

Fifth, adults bring problems to be solved to the Sunday morning classroom, whether or not they choose to share them with you or the class. The world is a complex place, and even if you (as teacher) don't have any idea of the issues with which they struggle, you can be sure they will be working at them as your ideas generate new thoughts, and they will be grateful for the opportunity.

Sunday morning offers a splendid opportunity for adult education, and the ways and means of organizing the time follow next.

MAKE ADULT EDUCATION INTERESTING

As a result of Sunday study, adults hope to carry home from church something that helps them see themselves and their world a bit differently. When this does not happen, they lean toward boredom, and, still later, quiet disappointment frequently encourages them to drop out.

Asked for ideas about subjects that interest them, many adults name topics like the following:

—Basic Bible 101. Most adults don't want advanced theology, and they don't want the Bible presented in the abstract. They want the Bible to touch their lives and make a difference where they live. They also want theological answers to questions like these:
—Why do bad things happen to good people?
—What makes one religion different from another?
—What makes our denomination unique?

Personal issues are also at the top of their list of interests, issues like these:

—Learning to parent the small child
—Learning to love to live with teenagers
—Death and dying
—Learning to manage stress

Short-term courses, like those provided by the seasonal approach suggested in this book and *Creative Christian Education*, provide the possibility for the specific focus that adults enjoy. And if there is sufficient interest in one six-week term's exploration, it can be easily continued into the next term. Please see Part IV of *CEME* for more ideas about topics for adults.

MAKING PLANS TO TEACH ADULTS

Adult programs ought to be planned before the year begins and published for all to see, and their inclusion in the parish program calendar is just the right place for them to be seen. A sample work sheet to help you make a program calendar for your parish is shown in illustration 13.

Teaching adults is made simple when we break the task up into manageable steps. For a more precise work sheet to help you construct a lesson plan, see illustration 16, "Sample work sheet: plan one Sunday."

1. *Get the attention* of your class in a personal way. Don't just begin by saying, "Today we will look of chapter 2 of 1 Corinthians." Make your beginnings personal, take care of housekeeping details, and inquire about any leftover responses from the previous Sunday's class. If someone was absent, welcome them back.

2. Next, *focus class attention* by welcoming today as a new possibility to learn, and be specific about this. If for example you are studying the Bible story of Abraham's commitment to sacrifice his son Isaac, state what personal need this story meets in our lives today. A brief statement helps make this focus explicit. Or ask a question and invite the brief response of your class. But by all means, invite them in to the exploration at this early moment, or they will go one way while you go another.

3. *Expand* the focus. This will be the bulk of your class. To continue with the story from Abraham's life, discussion might center on the anxiousness engendered when we walk by intuition or faith, hoping that what we are doing is right, although in the moment there are few, if any, assurances.

4. Finally, *celebrate* what you have just explored. A well-framed question will get this discussion off the ground and so will a question and answer period or a role play.

POINT FOR EDUCATION. Don't simply lecture to adults, and by all means never lecture to teens. The lecture format is an excellent way to get across a large body of information, but it is only one way among many. The model classroom will include not only lecture, but discussion, time for questions and answers, panel presentations and discussion, role play, films and other audio visuals.

Remember this when you begin to prepare for a stimulating class: We tend to remember something like

30 percent of what we hear,
40 percent of what we see, and
90 percent of what we do.

When you plan your teaching with this in mind, you will be off to a good start in education with both teenagers and adults.

WORKING WITH TEENAGERS: HOW TO PROCEED

What does a Sunday morning teenage classroom look like? The uninitiated may fear that it will look like bedlam, and to be sure, there is a lot of energy present. But embedded in this energy are teen hopes that their lives, interests, and issues will be valued in the Sunday morning setting.

Teenagers also want to know about God. But most of all they want to celebrate their lives and a broad personal future that seems to stretch forever. If you remember these three items and honor them all, you will be off to a good start.

In short, teenagers are fun to work with. They tend to ask a lot of honest questions, and their capacity to wrestle with really important issues is a joy. Each of the chapters in Part IV of *CEME* includes a section suggesting seasonal topics and themes likely to interest teens. Many are also appropriate for use in evening youth group settings.

"So," you say, "show me where to be begin." *First*, recognize that there's a big difference between the ages of thirteen and fourteen, and between the ages of eighteen and nineteen. In the small church setting where everyone knows everyone else, these groups can be combined. But in a large church setting this simply will not work.

Second, to prepare for your first class in September, find a quiet place where your class can meet and talk together. There should be a sense of privacy. Remember also to recognize that your class members will need to catch up on what happened over the course of the summer, and don't forget that while they do this they offer to one another important care. So don't interfere. Just be there and enter into the conversation when the opportunity presents itself. If you listen closely you'll hear all kinds of issues that will lend themselves to address during the year, so keep a mental list.

POINT. An opportunity to share personal stories and issues (and it will often sound like gossip) is a good way to begin every class every Sunday of the year for this reason: When you show teens that you value developing their capacity to work through their own issues, they will continue to knock at your door for a relationship.

One large parish has an open assembly for their teenage members. It is not a classroom, and if teens want classroom learning they are more than welcome in the adult classes. Many take advantage of the adult education programs, but more than a few choose the assembly. There they end up talking about things that matter to them over colas, coffee, and a donut or two (for sale by the youth group). Communion results, and I venture that the spirit of this event is one that God values as holy.

Third, be prepared to form a contract with your class. Now don't use this word with them, but be aware that—inevitably—you and they will enter into a contracting or covenanting period that, if well handled, will guarantee success for the year.

Here's what to expect. At some point in your first class session or second meeting (depending on how fast their energy to "catch up" is vented), some (or maybe just one) in the group will ask what this class will be doing for the rest of the year. This is a gold-mine time, for at precisely this point their interest is beginning to mesh with your interest. Move carefully, and here's how to proceed.

Be clear that the class is a joint effort, and be equally clear that you want to honor, not only your hopes for the year, but their hopes as well. So ask them what they'd like to cover, also tell them what you'd like to do, and then spend time figuring out the balance. You might also share with your class the mental list of issues you made during their earlier discussion and ask them to list in the order of importance each issue. With your additions and emendations, this list can become the agenda for the whole year. See how easy it is?

This covenanting or contracting period may not be completed in the first class session, and it might continue to appear now and then for the next few Sundays. But each time it does, talk about hopes and goals again.

POINT. If you simply impose your hopes and goals on a class of teenagers, resistance will build as surely as the sun rises every morning.

Fourth, as much as anything else, teenagers like the free-wheeling discussion that often takes shape each time the class gathers. But many adults are more than a little apprehensive that they will be called on to give answers that they don't have (as if any of us have all the answers).

Don't worry about giving answers, just listen to their discussion and note the issues that elicit their attention. Next, listen for the story that is inevitably attached to every issue, for these stories provide an excellent entrance into a discussion of God's ministry and their lives. Chapters 6 through 9 provide all you'll ever need to help these Christians wrestle with their questions about who God is and who they are, and they will be particularly appreciative if you help them begin with stories from their lives.

You can use well-developed lesson plans if you want, but because of what goes on in the public school during the week, their chance of succeeding is pale when measured against listening to the stories and events in which they are involved and using them as the basis for any discussion.

Still, you may want ideas, and until immediate help is handy you may be feeling a bit alone. Widely used and excellent resources are published by the Zondervan Publishing House, Grand Rapids, Michigan. Their "Youth Specialties" series lists titles like *Far Out Ideas, Holiday Ideas, Way Out Ideas, Ideas For Social Action,* and *Tension Getters.* If you need practical suggestions for either your Sunday morning class or the evening youth group, you will probably find them here. Please see appendix A for the address of the Zondervan Publishing House.

TROUBLESHOOTING YOUR WORK WITH TEENS

1. Teenagers expect adult leaders to be interested in them as persons, not children. When they don't get this kind of interest, they will act out or leave.

2. Teenagers have a lot going on in their lives, and the Sunday morning class must help them take care of their needs to talk about what's going on in their world before study gets serious. Often, a time to share with one another on Sunday morning—in an informal setting—is the very best way to work with teenagers.

3. Study sessions must be relaxed and fun, and humor is an important ingredient.

4. Teenagers are ready to engage in Bible study in depth if they are given an opportunity to formulate their questions, ask their

questions, and wrestle with finding their answers. The "Good News Method" of telling Bible stories offers this (chapter 6). So does gospel drama (chapter 8), and so does an exploration of stories from the here-and-now of their lives today (chapter 9).

5. Adult leaders must be candid. If you don't know what to say, say that, and invite your class to help you think things through. Better yet, help them come up with their own answers. This is the way they clarify their thoughts. But don't hide your own perspective and expect them to argue with you.

6. If members of your class "get out of line," don't take it personally unless you are breaking these guidelines. But if some do begin to act out, stop the class and talk about it. Teenagers, unless they are seriously disturbed will, if given an opportunity, enforce a compassionate law and order on one another.

7. If as an adult leader you expect a lot of "strokes" from teens, you will be likely disappointed. Strokes will come, but they will not come very rapidly until a relationship is built.

8. Only exceptional teachers can lecture teens for more than a few minutes and get away with it, if there is no test for graduation to be given.

One final word about success. If you feel like you're in trouble with your class, if there is more acting out than you can tolerate, or if things aren't going as you had hoped, get an outside consultation. Don't put it off. You are too important and so is your class.

Talk with your pastor or priest, a school teacher or principal you trust, or a parent who seems to have a special rapport with teens. Be prepared to tell them how you began the year, what you hoped for, and why you are now disappointed. Talking things out is old-fashioned advice that really works, and you will likely gain from this conversation new perspectives and new enthusiasm.

THE BOTTOM LINE: FAITH DEVELOPMENT FOR ADULTS AND TEENS

In the final analysis, just as we learned in chapter 3, Christian education for adults and teens is first of all interested in developing a mature Christian faith, and discussions of the sort suggested in this chapter are designed to do exactly that.

PART II

Planning to Use Bible Stories

CHAPTER FIVE

Planning the Year and Using the Bible

Good teaching always asks questions, and I like to begin every class with a question designed to hook interest. Often I'm surprised by what I hear, and this day was no exception.

To get my class in gear, right at the start I asked how many Bible stories a Sunday school class should study every year. Hardly a second passed before a hand shot up in the back of the room. "Seventy-two," said a former Sunday school superintendent and, at the time, a student at Virginia Seminary.

I was jolted by his enthusiasm, but catching my breath I asked how he arrived at such a figure. "I just took nine months, multiplied that number by four Sundays in each month, and figured that since we could learn two Bible stories each Sunday, I multiplied that number by two. The answer is seventy-two." He was quite pleased. I was, of course, less so.

Given the fact that we Sunday school teachers meet with our students only once a week and share with them only thirty-plus minutes of quality time, the goal posed by this enthusiastic student is unrealistic. Still, it's a goal that often seems to be adopted when some folks organize their parish for Christian education. But should you choose the approach he suggests, your children will be exhausted and your teachers wrecked.

I countered his seventy-two by suggesting that if I could help my parish explore just three or four Bible stories every year I would be satisfied.

By this point in *CEME* you have some idea about the importance and the ways and means to organize your parish for Christian education. You also know that it does not consist of studying seventy-two Bible stories. This chapter builds on the work begun in Part I and becomes even more explicit about making plans.

SETTING A PACE FOR LEARNING

No matter how you organize the nine-month Sunday school year, you're going to want to know how to fill each Sunday with good teaching and learning.

Partly at issue in this chapter is the task of pacing Sunday morning's nine-month educational journey. But just how do we determine how much we can learn over the course of a year? As noted in chapter 1, both *CEME* and *Creative Christian Education* answer this dilemma by suggesting a series of five terms, each about six weeks long and based on the historic Christian year.

Beginning in September with the

—All Saints term, the nine-month school year continues with a
—Christmas term, adds a term to cover the
—Epiphany season, includes a
—Lenten term, and ends the nine-month school year with an
—Easter/Pentecost term.

For example, during the All Saints term you can build a play about the life of a Bible character who was a saint of God, or Christians in other ages who loved the Lord and let it show in their lives. Stories about a few of these persons are found in the description of the Lenten term in Part IV of *CEME*.

The Christmas term lends itself to one or more Christmas pageants. But remember this: The play is not the most important thing; most important is the communion of putting the play together and sharing in joint tasks (like costuming, sets, banners, etc.).

Epiphany's theme of light means looking for stories like those of Jesus bringing light to his world, or women and men from church history who brought light to the world in their generation.

POINT. Let each term's theme guide you in your search for stories and personalities, and use gospel drama to make your classroom the most exciting place to be on Sunday morning.

6. Completed Work Sheet: planning the whole year
Elementary school children in a small parish or mission
by
Jim, Joy, and Carolyn

Season/Dates	Team members who will teach during this term	Your focus	Resources and activities to make the learning fun
ALL SAINTS	To celebrate our places in the Family of God		
Starting Date: 9-11-88 Ending Date: 10-23-88 Number of Sundays: 8 Festival Date: 10-30-88	Jim, Joy, & Carolyn	Saints who bring health and healing	*Bible Story:* Mark 9:14-29 *Song:* "I Sing a Song of the Saints" *Memory Verse:* Mark 9:37 *Activities:* Invite saints to visit. Make costumes for All Saints parade.
CHRISTMAS			
Starting Date: 11-6-88 Ending Date: 12-18-88 Number of Sundays: 8 Festival Date: 12-25-88	Joy & Carolyn	Special babies: Moses, Jesus, us	*Bible Story:* Exod. 2:1-10 *Song:* "Moses in the Bulrushes" *Memory Verse:* Luke 10:20 *Activities:* Chrismons; Moses pageant; bulletin board of us as babies.
EPIPHANY			
Starting Date: 1-1-89 Ending Date: 1-29-89 Number of Sundays: 6 Festival Date: 2-5-89	Carolyn & Jim	Sharing God's love with others— The Church's ministry	*Memory Verse:* Mark 16:15— The Great Commission *Song:* Hymn #528—"Lord, You give the Great Commission" *Activities:* Field trips exploring opportunities for ministry; banner making; Service of Commissioning.
LENT			
Starting Date: 2-12-89 Ending Date: 3-19-89 Number of Sundays: 6 Festival Date: 3-26-89	Jim & Joy	Preparation for Easter, using the Old Testament	*Bible Story:* Exod. 3:1-15— Moses' Call *Song:* "Go Down, Moses" *Memory Verse:* John 8:32 *Activities:* Puppet shows about today's outcasts.
EASTER/PENTECOST			
Starting Date: 3-26-89 Ending Date: 5-14-89 Number of Sundays: 8 Festival Date: 5-21-89	Joy & Carolyn	Fulfillment in Jesus	*Bible Story:* John 20:19-31 *Memory Verse:* John 20:31b *Activities:* Stop-action scenes; chancel drama with costumes and scenery.

By now you can plainly see how this schedule works to generate a pace for teaching and learning. Moreover, because these terms are based on the flow and movement of the historic church year, with all its festivals, Bible readings and color, choosing just one Bible story for study over the course of six weeks is as natural as day following the night.

The year's schedule developed by Carolyn, Jim and Joy, shown in illustration 6, includes an exploration of five Bible stories, notes a list of hymns to be learned, Bible verses to be memorized, and activities to be enjoyed. It's easy to plan a nine-month Sunday school year, and a sample work sheet to make it easy for you is included in this book (see illustration 15).

PLANNING TO USE THE BIBLE

Your plans for nine months ought always to include an exploration of a few Bible stories about God's action in life.

At fundamental levels we have to be honest with ourselves and with our tradition: Over the course of almost two thousand years God has met and been met by Christians through the pages of the Bible. If there were no Bible, we would neither know God consciously nor know that we are the people of God.

Now, there are bunches of other materials you can choose to use. Just a few are illustrated by Carolyn, Jim, and Joy, and still more suggestions are found in Part IV of *CEME*. But Bible stories help Christians meet and come to know God as no other means does.

USE JUST ONE BIBLE STORY FOR SEVERAL WEEKS

"But one Bible story for several weeks! Come on!" Even if you agree with me about the importance of Bible stories in Sunday morning Christian education, you might still be wondering how to cover a story given the brief time that Sunday morning provides us, and be still more incredulous with the idea of using the same story for several weeks.

Because we have only a few minutes to work on any Sunday morning, pick just one Bible story for study in each of the five terms proposed in *Creative Christian Education*. In other words, for six weeks explore just one Bible story. You can pick more than one, but the next few chapters will show you that more than one story is likely to be one story too many.

POINT. Always remember this: when planning your Sunday morning schedule, less is more. In other words, bite off less and have more fun. Part II in *CEME* is designed to show you how to put this idea to work.

MAKING BIBLE STORY VIDEOS

Don't make the mistake of thinking that the best Bible story resources are to be found in large musty Bibles written in an old English, Spanish, or oriental tongue. What we now call ancient writings were good for ancient people, but not so good for our classrooms today.

Most every church publishing house lists a number of Bibles translated and written for either children, teens, or adults. Some of these books have pictures, but every one of them pays close attention to making the Bible's stories easy to understand. In fact, there are also videos of Bible stories, and Arch Book videos are some of the best available. (See the bookstore appendix for details.)

Or more, every time you create a classroom drama to share with your parish, save it on video, catalog it in your parish library, and in just a few years you'll have quite a collection. And here is an added bonus; Videos like these also preserve the "people history" of your church, and although all of us grow old from child to adult, the video camera records forever the way it was . Should you try this approach, you will probably find that your homegrown video library is one of the most valued and often used collections in your library.

IF POSSIBLE, PLAN TOGETHER

More than anything else, loneliness destroys the enthusiasm that many teachers bring to the Sunday morning classroom. So if at all possible, make plans with one another. Two or more friendly heads are always better than one, and planning is always more satisfying when we are able to bounce our ideas off one another. The teaching schedule of Anne, Carolyn, Kathy, and Bonnie (see illustration 7) shows still another team's schedule for the nine-month school year.

POINT. I like to encourage the development of teaching teams. Most of us enjoy our work best when we are doing it with others. In addition, many men and women are involved in work-for-pay jobs during the five-day work week, and they are simply unable to

7. One year's teaching schedule

YEAR'S TEACHING SCHEDULE, GRADES 4 & 5
TEAM: Carolyn, Anne, Kathy, Bonnie

TERM'S THEME	MAJOR TEACHERS	RESOURCES
All Saints: Jacob	Carolyn, Anne (Kathy & Bonnie out)	Parents assist with drama, others with banner making
Christmas: Light coming into the world as seen in worship and our use of bread, study of symbols	Carolyn, Anne, Kathy (Bonnie out)	Parishioner breadmaker help; parents help with Chrismons
Epiphany: Drama: Amahl and the Night Visitors, Second half, Jesus' boyhood	Parents help with drama. Kathy, Bonnie, Carolyn lead study of boyhood (Anne out)	Organist, a carpenter visits, trip to synagogue, slides on Palestine.
Lent: Jesus' ministry. Death. New life. Seeds and Easter egg tree.	Bonnie, Anne, Kathy (Carolyn out)	Puppet show on death. Parent help with Easter eggs.
Easter/Pentecost: Parables of Jesus	Carolyn, Kathy (Anne & Bonnie out)	Flower planting, stick puppets, dioramas

From CREATIVE CHRISTIAN EDUCATION, *p. 81.*

commit themselves to a primary teaching responsibility for a nine-month period.

When teaching teams are carefully developed, supported, and used, they offer an answer to loneliness that makes all kinds of good sense. In a small church Sunday school program the teaching team may well consist of a good portion of the Sunday school itself.

YOUR INTEREST IS MOST DEAR

Finally, when you select a Bible story, value your own interest as the most important asset. Also, remember to pick a story and not an abstract lesson. A *story* of love, like that of the Good Samaritan, is far more effective in the Sunday morning classroom than a treatise or *lesson* on love, like that found in 1 Corinthians 13.

Stories also help keep classroom learning concrete, a particularly important point when working with younger children. What is more, once you begin to explore a story with older classes, their interest will naturally generate questions and discussions of interest to them.

> A teacher recently reported to me that one of his students moaned when he announced the morning's exploration. "I'm not interested in that," said the young man. "Why not?" asked his teacher. "Because I'm not," was the reply of his young charge.
>
> "Well *I am interested* because this is a very good story about God," said the teacher, and it was said with such conviction that the class immediately began to follow where he led.

Good teaching provides good leadership, and good leadership is built upon enthusiasm for the task at hand. I hope you'll commit to using a few Bible stories every year, and use the ideas in parts II and III of *CEME* to make the kinds of plans that keep enthusiasm high and satisfaction sturdy.

CHAPTER SIX

Discover God in Action: An Easy-to-Use Method of Bible Study

People want to know more about God—not just ideas about God, but the shape of God's action in the midst of everyday life. "What difference does God make?" Christians ask. The "Good News Method" of Bible study presented in this chapter is constructed to answer this question. Because it centers its attention on the good news perspectives of God's action, it generates enthusiasm in all age groups. Moreover, because many Sunday school teachers fear using the Bible, this may be *CEME's* most important chapter.

DON'T PUT OUT THE SPIRIT'S FIRE

The whole point of Bible study is to learn about God—not just God's action in the past, but God's action in our lives today. This kind of Bible study sets modern day hearts on fire, for it presents good news that the world longs to hear.

The Christian gospel, or good news, is simply this: We are made by God for life, health, and wholeness. We are not made for destruction and death. And in Jesus' life, death, and resurrection, we are privileged to catch a vision of this promise of God.

Every Bible story has a core point of good news about God's action, and this perspective becomes explicit the more we pay attention to the feelings that Bible stories generate in us. So when you explore stories from the Bible, look for gospel feelings.

What are gospel feelings? We get a gospel feeling after we close our eyes for a long period of time, feel the impotence of being unable to see, and then open our eyes to the world about us. Close your eyes right now and keep them closed for a minute. Then open them and watch the shapes and colors jump out at you. With your eyes closed you probably felt a bit like you were imprisoned; with them open there's a feeling of freedom.

Gospel is also the good news feeling one gets after having hobbled about on a crutch and then finding it "really can" be put away. Gospel is the feeling emerging as one hears, "Well done," after having completed a very difficult task (Matt. 25:21, 23).

The feeling of gospel has to do with being noticed and set free by God and the satisfaction, peace, acceptance, and enthusiasm that results. Some folks got a gospel feeling everyplace that Jesus went, and it changed their lives forever.

POINT. Bible stories provide a classroom environment in which God's gospel of life can be engaged at both feeling and thinking levels, and as a result we have every reason to expect Christian faith to grow toward maturation.

The following Bible stories briefly illustrate gospel feelings. Remember, we are not about the task of offering our student's high-powered and academic theological education. We are about the task of helping God and God's people meet, using stories from Scripture of God's mighty acts in the past.

Blind Bartimaeus (Mark 10:46-52), a pushy man, got what he wanted, his sight, because he asked. What did he think as his eyes first opened, and how did long-closed eyes feel when they saw the face of the man who gave them sight? Here are gospel feelings.

I wonder how the lame man felt as his friends gathered him up on a bed, took him to a house in which Jesus was meeting, only to discover they couldn't move near the One who might help (Luke 5:18-26). That's bad news, like hell.

I wonder how his feelings began to change when those same friends discovered the outside staircase to the roof. But I wonder most what he thought and felt when he heard the words, "Rise . . . and walk," and what he felt as a result. That's gospel.

Wonder with your children how Jairus—an important ruler of the synagogue—felt, knowing his small daughter was dying (Luke 8:40-42, 49-56).

And then wonder about the change in his thoughts and feelings when he heard she was going to be alright.[1]

The "Good News Method" of telling Bible stories presented in this chapter pays close attention to gospel feelings, and the following illustrations show the incredible power present when Bible stories are presented in this fashion. A work sheet to help you use this method is shown in illustration 8.

8. Work Sheet: Making easy plans to tell a Bible story

Remembering that "less is more" in the Sunday morning classroom, think about using *one* Bible story for a whole term. Here's how: Simply divide the number of weeks in the term in half. Then in the first half treat the story as a there-and-then picture of God's ministry in the past, and in the second half paint a here-and-now picture of this same godly ministry in our lives today. Of course, depending upon your interest you might want to focus not equal attention on both foci, but weight your focus toward one direction or another.

Remember: What interests and excites you will interest and excite your students.

STEP 1: Developing the there-and-then perspective. Every Bible story paints a picture of God at work in God's world, and since the Bible is written about long ago events, this first step develops a there-and-then picture of God at work in the world.

1. Refer to the lectionary and pick a story for the term you are planning. Read the story through, but keep a sharp eye out for *signs of God's ministry.* Underline *action words that paint a picture of God's ministry.* Use your imagination, and remember that God is always working to *make things new,* bringing what is dead to life, helping the blind see, the deaf hear, the crippled walk, and setting the captives free (Luke 4:16-21). The "Good News Method" always looks for God's *"making things new"* ministry.

2. Before moving to the here-and-now of life today, stop and make a play of the story. Or create a picture or banner of it, or do any one of a number of arts and crafts activities suggested in this chapter.

   POINT. Tasks and activities help us explore the story further, and each minute it is further explored, the more opportunity God has to say, "It's true." Consider developing a *traditional pageant, a scene or shadow play, congregational drama,* or use *gospel drama* (described in a later chapter).

STEP 2. Having explored the there-and-then of the Bible story, we are now free to move to the here-and-now of God's action in life today. The following generic questions are designed to help focus your planning. They are also designed to help strengthen congregational life.

1. Because the human condition never changes, what conditions shown in the story appear in our lives today? Pick several areas that pique your interest, and choose one to explore.

2. Because God never changes, where and how do you see God stirring, enlightening, and strengthening us to help him take action in these similar events today? Particularly,

   —How is your parish at work supporting this work of God in your community or the world?

   —How is your denomination at work in this same field of endeavor?

   —How is God mobilizing your local community to take action in behalf of those who need help?

STEP 3. Finally, and if you have not already done so, celebrate both there-and-then and here-and-now perspectives with classroom tasks and craft activities. Make use of the suggestions offered in chapter 6 and chapter 7.

INTRODUCING THE GOOD NEWS METHOD OF TELLING BIBLE STORIES

"The Good News Method" of Bible study makes use of three steps, and they take the following order. This method

1. develops a there-and-then perspective that celebrates God's presence and ministry in the story itself, it makes a play of the story, then it

2. identifies these same signs of God's ministry in the here-and-now of our lives today, and finally it

3. celebrates what we are learning with crafts and tasks.

To show you how the "Good News Method" works with an actual Bible story, let's look at the Hebrew Bible's account of David and Goliath (1 Samuel 17). But don't read this story from the Bible yet. First, explore how the "Good News Method" will treat it, and then read it.

First, this there-and-then Bible story shows *God at work stirring the heart and interest* of a shepherd boy to take care of his country. This sets the "Good News Method" apart from all others: It looks for actual signs of God's presence and ministry.

Look at the turning points: David decides to leave his flock and visit his family; he overhears talk of Goliath; he listens to his brothers; and he decides to act. "Why did he do all this?" the Christian wonders. And, "Is it only because of his own good heart, or do we see here signs of the ministry of Another?" The Bible says the latter.

This short story can next be made into any one of several kinds of plays listed later in this chapter, and while the play is being constructed, the story will easily be learned and remembered and questions about God generated.

Second, it follows naturally to look for similarities between this story and the here-and-now of life today. For instance, who are the "Goliaths" we face in today's world? Drugs. Pressures to grow up too quickly and succeed in a perform-ance-valuing world. Alcohol. A lack of self-esteem. High-powered job expectations that push us to "succeed" while sacrificing family life. *How is God,* directly and through the church, *helping us meet these Goliaths?* Moreover, who are the "Davids" who offer care for us today?

Third and finally, make a banner, video, or any number of crafts and activities to celebrate both this story and what you are learning. And be prepared to present some of this at the term-ending show-and-tell festival.

Now read the story of David and Goliath (1 Samuel 17), and see how Bible stories come to life when approached by the "Good News Method." And remember this: When something is experienced,

we understand it more,

we remember it better, and

we're compelled to proceed with further questions.

GOOD NEWS STORYTELLING GUIDELINES: IN DETAIL

The "Good News Method" employs a sensitivity toward what every Bible story says about God. It does not ignore the human dimensions in the story, but most of all it values *God's love and ministry* in action.

POINT. A work sheet to help you use the "Good News Method" of telling Bible stories is shown in illustration 8. When using it, consider the following perspectives.

STEP 1. Consider what the story says about God's there-and-then love long ago. *Identify God's ministry* by asking a question like this one; "What signs can I see of God's action?" Every story in the Bible is a story about God, so look for *turning points* and good news perspectives that show *God in action.*

The Episcopal Book of Common Prayer (p. 858) says that God *enlightens* our minds (gives us a better idea), *stirs* our hearts (to new possibilities), and *strengthens* our wills (to follow through even when the going gets tough).

But God also takes into account human freedom (the Prayer Book, p. 845), and the truth is that because of our freedom we often sabotage God's hopes for us. So when you look for turning points, pay attention to the way in which God works with human freedom. For example, David was free to listen to God's nudgings or not, and if he had not, things would have been a good deal different.

Still, God doesn't desert us but always works to *make things new*, bringing what is dead to life, helping the blind see, the deaf hear, the crippled walk, and setting the captives free (Luke 4:16-21). The "Good News Method" always looks for God's *"making things new"* ministry.

POINT. Look for *turning points* when the action of the story could have gone one way and not another, and speculate on God's "stirring a new idea ministry" in the background.

With these perspectives in mind, now make the story into a brief play. When I use the "Good News Method," I like to introduce the story itself by constructing a play. This makes Bible study a lot more fun and means that students will raise questions naturally as the play is being constructed.

When questions arise (that both students and I generate) I pause for discussion.

POINT. This method of Bible study isn't interested in simply constructing a play, as much fun as that is. First of all, it is designed to involve students in a Bible story so that they can meet and be met by God.

Four easy ways to make plays are described later in this chapter.

STEP 2. Next, consider the way in which these same good news perspectives help us see God's love in the here-and-now of our lives today. If at all possible I like to ground this discussion in the ministry of my parish to God's world. Such an approach strengthens the church.

Discerning these parish good news perspectives is greatly helped by the use of the following *generic* questions. Not all of these inquiries will be applicable to every Bible story, but in most cases all will stand you in good stead.

Because God never changes, how is *God showing* this same quality of Bible care in our lives (your life) today? Particularly,

    a) How is *God acting to provide* this same quality of love and care in the ministry of your congregation to the community?

    b) How is *God acting to provide* this same quality of love and care in your denomination's ministry to our country and the world?

c) How is *God acting to provide* this same quality of love and care through your daily occupations (and the occupations of others) everywhere they work? All of us help God take care of God's world.

d) If God's displeasure is present, look behind it to see why. God is always angry when we abuse the covenant relationship he has with us and when we abuse one another. If God is standing over against selfishness and self-centeredness in the story, how is God doing the same thing in our corporate lives today? So whenever you see God's anger, look behind it to see the abuse present. Then look for the better way for which God is also working.

Let's return to the story of David and Goliath and look for some of the here-and-now perspectives.

One Goliath our children face in the world is *drug abuse.* It seems to be taking over, and both the church and modern culture are beginning to take action. Educational programs are being constructed, family life is being attended as never before, and government resources are being applied. God is at work, and though you won't hear this fact mentioned in the morning newspaper, to eyes of faith signs of God's care are obvious.

POINT. This is the reason we use Bible stories in the Sunday morning classroom: The world will not hear of God in the daily newspaper.

If you are working with teenagers, ask them to describe the Goliaths they face, and then explore for the ways in which God is stirring the church to action.

But is the church doing all we can be doing? Interview parishioners about what actions they think we need to be taking. Next, help your teenage class construct a program in response, and with a hope for adoption, present their program to your church governing body.

With smaller children, be prepared to guide their thinking with practical suggestions. For example, God stirs the interest of their teachers and principal to help them understand the consequences of the use of drugs.

Two more illustrations of here-and-now perspectives might help your vision take firm shape. If you are studying the parable of the *Good Samaritan* (Luke 10:33f.), who of the characters in this story best represents God and/or the church? Who are the beaten in our culture who are receiving God's and/or the church's attention? What signs do you see of this, and how can the church more ably assist God's ministry of care? Or, if you are studying the story of *Daniel in the den of the lions* (Dan. 6:1-23), who are the lions in the lives of your students or in your community and the world? How does your parish tame them and shut their mouths for the sake of justice and peace?

STEP 3. Finally, and this is a crucial part of the "Good News Method," celebrate what you are learning with a classroom task or craft activity. Don't put out the Spirit's fire, for God uses the joy of times like these to burn the truth of his love on hearts now turned to him (though I'll confess "hearts turned to God" is not an apt description of some children on some mornings).

The following four lists are sure to contain several suggestions that interest you, and each one has proven a helpful aid in the Sunday morning classroom.

ART:

Banners (of the story itself or what you discover of God's love today)
Bulletin board
Carvings
Cartoons
Castings
Collages
Crayon drawings
Decoupage
Dolls
Drawing
Dyeing
Masks
Mobiles
Models
Montages
Murals
Paintings
Papier-mâché
Plaques
Posters
Prints and printing
Rubbings

Sculptures
Sewing
Slides (write-on and photo)
Stenciling
Weaving
Wire sculptures
Woodworking

PLAYS (described in this and later chapters):
Gospel drama (described in Part II of *CEME*)

Walk-through-life with God drama (described in Part II of *CEME*)
Pageants
Scene plays
Shadow plays
Congregational drama
Videos

ACTION:
Camera/taking pictures
Dance
Field trips

Motion pictures
Pantomime
Photography
Puzzles
Service projects
TALKING:
Choral reading
Conversation/discussion
Drama/skits/stories
Interview parishioners and/or
    other students
Puppets
Role playing

Storytelling
WRITING:
Chancel play (to be presented
    in church)
Drama (narrated in the class-
    room)
Filmstrip series
Letters (to the shut-in you
    adopted)
Litany
Poetry
Prayers
Stories

POINT. God is always about the task of caring about the world in identifiable ways, and both parish life and Christian faith are strengthened when we become particularly clear about the way in which God is with us.

MOBILIZING YOUR CONGREGATION TO HELP

Many programs of Christian education go wrong because they don't ask enough of the parish. Conduct a parishwide preregistration in the spring and a registration in the fall, using as a point of reference the discussion of registration in chapter 7 of *Creative Christian Education*, "September Start-up: The Practical Details." Then you will know right off the bat that a lot of parishioners would love to be involved, if they can use their particular skills in certain tasks and if they don't have to commit to teaching every Sunday.

Right from the beginning, as you make plans for the year and begin to think of some of the tasks you want to accomplish, select some of these folks and ask them to take a responsibility. For example, they could learn how to implement some of the arts and crafts activities just noted, develop simple-to-use procedures to put to work the four kinds of drama described next in this chapter, or help particular classes with the arts and crafts activities noted in the next chapter.

I can see resource specialists becoming skilled in helping classes learn to identify God's action in Bible stories, while still others hone the skill of helping classes identify God's action in the ministry of your parish.

Also ask one or two of these good-hearted volunteers to develop their capacity to introduce and work with the ideas presented in "Gospel Drama" (chap. 8) and "Learning to Speak of God in Today's World" (chap. 9).

If you are enthusiastic about your Sunday morning program, so will be other Christians. And they will be delighted to help you out if you need their help, and if they know what to do.

FOUR EASY WAYS TO MAKE BIBLE STORY PLAYS

Bible stories are not written because of what they say about human beings. They are written to show us *God at work* in the world. They show us many other things as well, but God's action is of first interest. Here's why. Bible writers knew full well that if God's actions were preserved for future generations, those generations would also come to love the same God who acts in the same way forever. Bible story plays celebrate just this point.

A Pageant

To construct a *pageant*, break any Bible story up into as many scenes as necessary and appoint a narrator(s). Add to the number of participants, if necessary, mainly because you may be working with more children than the Bible supplies parts. At some point you may wish to include a hymn or two or three and have the congregation sing them while the pageant pauses as a tableau.

The story of David and Goliath lends itself to pageant construction. How big will Goliath be, and what kind of costumes and sets will be constructed? As this play is prepared, the story itself is heard at deeper and deeper levels, and God is given an opportunity to show us that he cares for us in the same way today.

And don't forget this point:

We remember 10 percent of what we HEAR.
We remember 50 percent of what we SEE.
We remember 90 percent of what we DO.

A Scene Play

Constructing a *scene play* is also good teaching at its best, and every Bible story has several scenes awaiting to be identified by your imagination. In the story of David and Goliath, a first scene can show Goliath terrorizing the Hebrews; a second scene can show David with his sheep; a third scene shows David visiting his brothers; a fourth scene shows David offering himself; and a fifth scene shows him facing Goliath.

A scene play treats these scenes as photographs. So have everyone take places, carefully construct the first scene by positioning participants, exaggerate their facial expressions and gestures, and finally *freeze* the action. Now ask participants to remember exactly their places and appearances. A first scene is now in hand. Construct the rest in the same fashion.

When you present this scene play to others (maybe the shut-in your class adopted, another class, church, or the hospital pediatrics unit), ask the audience to be the stage curtain. This technique is perhaps a scene play's best component. Here's how this technique works. "Curtain down" means close your eyes, and "Curtain up" means open your eyes. Carefully practice this with your audience. Now you have a way to box each scene in with a curtain call. Everyone will have lots of fun.[1]

On the day of presentation, ready your actors and have the narrator begin to read the story. When the story gets to the first scene you've prepared, call for "curtain down." When the scene is ready for viewing call for "curtain up." Pause for a moment or two, read the next portion of the story, and when time for the next scene arrives, call for "curtain down." Repeat this process until the play is completed.

Remember:

> I hear and I forget.
> I see and I remember.
> I do and I understand.

A Shadow Play

A shadow play is simply a brief drama presented behind a sheet or a large semitransparent cloth. This allows the action to be seen without the need for special costuming. Imagination is teased by shadow plays in a way pageants and scene plays cannot, and shadow plays lend themselves to the presentation of several scenes.

Congregational Drama

Your class can also involve the entire congregation in stories from Scripture, and in their preparation God will have every opportunity to touch even more lives with the truth of his presence. Furthermore, in the process everyone will have a lot of fun and discover that the Bible really does "live" today as a witness to God's power.

Here's how to proceed with congregational drama. Read the story with your class and pick key words that describe the action of the story. Then attach to these key words a dramatic noise, like a *hooray* or say the word *sad* if the key word connotes sadness.

Let me illustrate this with the story of the paralyzed man brought to Jesus by his four friends (Mark 2:1-12). The key words in the story itself are designated by italics, and the noises and words attached to them are as follows. At the word *paralyzed*, the congregation says "Sad." At the name of Jesus, "ouoooooooo." At the word *crowd*, "wow." At *roof*, "uh-oh." And at *walk*, they say, "All right!"

Now the story.

> When after some days *Jesus* returned to Capernaum, the news went round that he was home; and such a *crowd* collected that the space in front of the door was not big enough to hold them. Now while *Jesus* was proclaiming the message to them, a man was brought who was *paralyzed*. Four men were carrying him, but because of the *crowd* they could not get near. So they opened up the *roof* over the place where *Jesus* was, and when they had broken through the *roof* they lowered the stretcher on which the *paralyzed* man was lying. When *Jesus* saw their faith, he said to the *paralyzed* man, "My son, your sins are forgiven."
>
> Now there were some lawyers sitting in the *crowd*, and they thought to themselves, "Why does this fellow talk like that? This is blasphemy. Who but God alone can forgive sins? Can *Jesus*? *Jesus* knew in his own mind that this was what they were thinking and said to them: "Why do you harbor thoughts like these? Is it easier to say to this *paralyzed* man 'Your sins are forgiven,' or to say 'Stand up, take up your bed and *walk*'? But to convince you that the Son of man has the right on earth to forgive sins"—he turned to the *paralyzed* man—"I say to you, stand up, take up your bed, and *walk*." And he got up, and at once took his stretcher and went out in full view of the *crowd*, so that all were astounded and praised God. Never before, said the *crowd*, have we seen the like of *Jesus*. (Mark 2:1-12 NEB)

To remind the congregation of their responses, print their parts on large placards, and when the appropriate word from the story is read, hold up the placard with their response. They will become one with the story, and I think you will find that the story is remembered far better than if it is just read once.

Congregational drama easily actualizes gospel feelings and good news perspectives.

THE GOOD NEWS METHOD IN ACTION: TEACHING THE STORY OF THE WIDOW'S MITE

The remaining two sections in this chapter are ready-to-use treatments of two Bible stories, using the "Good News Method." The story of the widow who gave her all is one of the grandest stories of love in all the Bible. Here's what happened.

> Jesus was standing outside the temple treasury watching as people dropped their money into the chest. Many of the rich gave large amounts and were noticed with favor. And then a poor widow dropped in two tiny coins, and Jesus called his disciples to him,
> "I tell you this," he said, "this poor widow has given more than any of the others; for those others who have given had more than enough, but she, with less than enough, has given all that she had to live on." (NEB Mark 12:41-44)

STEP 1. Look for signs of God's there-and-then action in this story.

At first glance all that seems to be seen of God's presence and ministry is shown by Jesus, and what we see is this: God does notice what we do, and God commends us when we care for him and for one another.

But more, this woman's love clearly evidences God's love toward us, and the love of Jesus for the world.

While others loved to brag, she was *stirred by God* to love extravagantly. And if her action represents what is good and decent in human beings, Jesus also uses her to illustrate *the shape of God's extravagant love for us.*

The "Good News Method" of telling Bible stories draws from Bible stories all that they can say about God.

But if extravagant love often marks human life, so too does jealousy. So when you see human beings beating up on one another (in this case, criticizing unfairly), look for signs of sin, human freedom, God's powerlessness, and the work of the Adversary of Scripture (see chapter 9).

Now make this story into a play or pageant, show it in a banner to be shared with your church, paint a picture of it; or sculpt it.

REMEMBER: If you are clearly interested in the arts and crafts activity, and if you value Bible stories as important vehicles to introduce the people of the world to God, so too will your children.

STEP 2. Now move from the Bible story's past to the here-and-now of life today. God never changes, and this Bible story tells us in word and picture what we can expect of God in our lives today.

    a) Where are signs of God's extravagant love that show in our lives today? For example, there is the love and care of parents and siblings for one another, daily bread on the table, and the work of your parish and denomination in the world. Which one of these areas of exploration interests you?

    b) If God is standing over against selfishness and self-centeredness in the story, how is God doing the same thing in our lives today? For example, in this story God shows his thoughts in Jesus' life, and Jesus is clearly displeased with those who brag or otherwise puff themselves up and lord it over others.

    God does not approve of bullies, nor those who give to others only to blow their own horns. They really care for no one but themselves. Now move in your thinking to the here-and-now of life today.

    QUESTION. When have your children been hurt by others who were puffed up at their expense? How has God acted in their behalf? Ask for personal stories, and if no godly action could be seen at the time, it was probably because God was powerless—no one was there to help God out. But know this also: God is now using this classroom event to redeem a painful memory and make things all right. For more perspectives on God's power and God's powerlessness, see chapter 9.

    c) Where is the church in this story? It is represented both by the woman and those who criticize her. How is your church, your denomination showing God's extravagant love in the world? Coffee hours and receptions, if not extravagant, do provide times for the celebration of affection and community. Christian education programs, Bible study groups, aerobic exercise classes, food pantries, a community soup kitchen, a Scout group, or perhaps community groups use your facilities for a place to meet—all are expressions of God's extravagant love.

    d) How is God showing this same quality of love and care in your denomination's ministry to our country and the world? Perhaps your denomination is at work helping alleviate world hunger, prejudice, or racism. But don't just name the ways, explore them in detail and always as an illustration of God's extravagant love for us.

STEP 3. Now celebrate God's action and/or your current ministry with arts and craft activities. Pick any one or more of the following tasks and learn even more about the love God first shows us in the

Bible story. Each one of these activities is discussed in Part II of *Creative Christian Education.*

—*Create a skit* about the way in which God's extravagant love shows up in our lives today. Maybe one of your children was stirred to "rescue" another child or a pet from danger or to intervene in a relationship for the sake of compassion and care. Simply make that event into a play, and be sure to include God as a participant as described in chapter 9, "Learning to Speak of God in Today's World."

—*Develop an intergenerational activity* event for one Sunday, and involve the whole parish in your exploration. See chapters 2 and 7 for ideas about intergenerational festivals.

—To show God's love today, *interview parishioners* and/or other students about the way in which your parish brings the extravagant light of God's love to God's world, paying particular attention to your ministry in your local community.

—*Create a video, motion picture film, or collage* of photographs showing the way in which your parish brings light to the world.

—*Write a litany* to celebrate the light your parish brings to God's world.

—*Design a banner* to show the way in which God's extravagant love shows forth in the world or your student's lives.

—*Create a bulletin board display* about the story your class explores and the activities you relate to it.

—Prepare to present the work of this term to *the shut-in* you've adopted, and be ready to make a home visit.

It doesn't take long to fill a six-week schedule. Notice how in each of these tasks the themes of the lessons are given clear expression. By the time the term is over, the story you have chosen will be well known and so will God's love.

THE GOOD NEWS METHOD IN ACTION: THE KING WHO PREPARED A WEDDING FEAST

Now let's turn to a final illustration of the "Good News Method" of Bible study. The parable Jesus told about a king who prepared a feast for his son's wedding provides the example.

The story goes like this:

> A king wanted to honor the marriage of his son with a feast, and after careful preparations he sent for those whom he had invited. But they did not come.

So the king again sent his servants to these same folks, and on this second visit his servants were beaten and killed.

Not to be outdone, still a third time the king sent his servants to invite a whole new set of folks to the celebration. This time guests came. But one was not dressed, and that one was cast out with anger. (condensed from Matt. 22:1-14)

This story is full of rich teaching themes, so the "Good News Method" of telling Bible stories asks this question first: What does this story show us of God's love and action in life?

First, the king represents God, and the story suggests that God is always calling us to a banquet. Second, God values us and expects the best from us. Happily, God also loves us when we fall short, but the vision is clear isn't it; God expects eyes-wide-open faithfulness from us and is always faithful to us.

Now let's develop these questions to help our class explore these good news perspectives and understand what it's like to be in God's shoes.

STEP 1. Looking for signs of God's there-and-then love in the past.

Suppose a king (president of the United States or any other in authority) invited folks to a party for his only child, a son of whom he was proud. And suppose those he invited made a joke of the invitation. What do you think should happen?

How would you dress if a king (president of the United States or any other in authority over you) invited you to a party for his only child, a son of whom he was proud. Would it occur to you to ask about appropriate attire, or would you expect the host to tell you what to wear?

Suppose one person came without the right attire to the most important party of the year. What should happen to him? Do you think the king had a reason to be mad? Next, create a scene play to dramatize this story.

STEP 2. Now move from the Bible story's past to the here-and-now of life today. God never changes, and this Bible story tells us in word and picture what we can expect of God in our lives today.

God is the king, and we have an invitation to his banquet. But what signs of God's banquet show in our lives today?

a) What signs of a God-provided banquet show today in your family life? Parental love and affection may be one such sign. But suppose there is little parental support for some of your children. Does this mean God is not interested? Look then for signs of the banquet in the support given by extended family members or important teachers (like you) or surrogate families (like the school or church or community organizations with which the child identifies). The point is this: God is always doing in our midst infinitely more than we can ask for or imagine, and Christian education at its best simply points this out.

b) How is God showing what may be called his banquet love in the life of your congregation?

God invites us to his Sunday school class so that we can meet him and one another. What have you been learning? What do you and your class look forward to on Sunday morning? Task: Make a banner to show the banquet of our class, write a litany of thanks, or make a play.

God invites us to be a part of the church, a fellowship of folks who believe he loves us. How does God show his love for us in this community? Interview parishioners. Why is the church important in the world? Why is our church important in this community? Task: Make a banner, write a litany, or put on a play.

c) How is God showing banquet love and care in the ministry of your congregation to the community?

d) How is God showing this same quality of love and care in our denomination's ministry to your country and the world?

e) How is God showing this same quality of love and care in our daily occupations (and the occupations of others) everywhere they work? All of us help God take care of God's world.

f) If God is standing over against selfishness and self-centeredness in the story, how is God doing the same thing in our corporate lives today?

NOTE. Jesus models the kind of eyes-wide-open faithfulness God expects from us. So do the saints of the church. Appropriate stories are suggested in the Lenten term of *Creative Christian Education.*

Moreover, church history, world history, and life today also suggest a host of people who model the eyes-wide-open faithfulness God expects from us. Suggestions are offered in the section "Others Who Dared: Church History," page 155 of *Creative Christian Education.*

STEP 3. Celebrate the story with arts and crafts activities.

—*Put on a skit* about the banquet your church sets before your local community, in God's name.

—*Interview parishioners* and/or other students about the banquet of parish life, past and present.

—*Create a video, motion picture film, or collage* of photographs portraying the work of your church today.

—Write a *litany* to celebrate the banquet you are studying.

—Create a *banner* to celebrate the banquet God provides you through the life of your parish.

—*Make posters* for hallway display.

Always look first for the good news message that every Bible story speaks of God, and begin to teach from that perspective. What stories say about human beings is OK, too. But what they say about God is better and infinitely more satisfying.

Given the few minutes we have on Sunday morning, here is Christian education at its best.

Notes

1. From Howard Hanchey, *Creative Christian Education* (Wilton, CT: Morehouse-Barlow, 1986), p. 134.

2. This snapshot method of presenting a play is widely used, but Tom Long and his *Friends of the Groom* (83 Gatch Street, Milford, OH 45150) have developed it and other methods into exciting gospel presentations. Tom and his company are more than happy to go "on the road." They have a fee scale, and if you want first-class help with telling Bible stories that make them unforgettable, ask Tom and his friends for help.

CHAPTER SEVEN

Matching Arts and Crafts with Bible Stories

Arts and crafts bring joy to the Sunday morning classroom. Indeed, they make learning fun, and when such activities are attached to the study of a Bible story, life in the Sunday morning classroom sings a song of satisfaction. This chapter picks a few of the suggestions made in chapter 6 and develops them with your congregation's life in mind.

Instead of enjoying activities like those noted in this chapter, many Sunday school programs "go wrong" by valuing the acquisition of more and more information and "facts," whatever these may be. The public school is their model of choice and, since these congregations, like the rest of us, have only thirty-plus minutes with which to work on Sunday morning, their programs quickly flounder on the rocks of student resentment or just plain non-attendance. There is a better way.

If you are feeling a bit fearful, however, on the order of "I'm not very creative," think about using other folks in the parish to develop each of the following activities. This idea is explained in the section of chapter 6 called "Mobilizing Your Congregation to Help."

But if you still want more help for yourself, be assured that there are more than a few books on the market designed to help you. Just a few of those available are found in appendix A, "A Bookstore for You."

DEVELOP HERE-AND-NOW PERSPECTIVES IN THE STUDY OF BIBLE STORIES

Celebrate God's action in life today. There-and-then perspectives in every Bible story invariably suggest here-and-now declarations, and the "Good News Method" of telling Bible stories uses this natural rhythm.

POINT. People yearn to hear more about God, and they want to know what difference God makes in their daily lives. Here-and-now perspectives are designed to show this difference and help people to talk about it.

For example, if you are studying the parable of the Good Samaritan (Luke 10:33f.), which of the characters in this story best represents God and/or the church? Who are the beaten in our culture *who are receiving God's and/or the church's attention*, and how can the church more ably assist God's ministry of care?

To develop these good news perspectives of God's love today, pay particular attention to the following *generic* questions. Not all of these questions will be applicable to every Bible story, but in most cases all will stand you in good stead.

1. God never changes. So now comes the question, How is *God showing* this same quality of Bible care in our lives (your life) today?

2. How is *God showing* this same quality of love and care in the ministry of our congregation to the community?

POINT. Every congregation has a ministry to the community in which it resides. But I am often surprised at how little many Christians know about the marks of their ministry today. This will change only by paying attention to the shape of current ministry and how present ministry is also an expression of ministry in the past. Sunday morning Christian education is precisely positioned to conduct this exploration.

3. How is *God showing* this same quality of love and care in our denomination's ministry to our country and the world?

4. How is *God showing* this same quality of love and care through our daily occupations (and the occupations of others) everywhere they work? All of us help God take care of God's world.

5. If God's displeasure is present, look behind it to see why. God is always angry when we abuse the covenant relationship he has with us and when we abuse one another. If God is standing over against selfishness and self-centeredness in the story, how is *God doing* the same thing in our corporate lives today? So whenever you see God's

anger, look behind it to see the abuse present. Then look for the better way for which *God is also working.*

The story of *David and Goliath* (I Samuel 17) also suggests many here-and-now perspectives. One "Goliath" our children face in the world is drug abuse. How is *God stirring* both church and society to take action? Educational programs are being constructed, family life is being attended as never before, and government resources are being applied. God is at work.

If you are working with teenagers, ask them to describe the Goliaths they face, and then explore for the ways in which *God is stirring* the church to action. Always focus on God's action. That's what Christians yearn to hear.

But is the church doing all it can be doing? Interview parishioners about what actions they think we need to be taking to support *God's already present action.*

With smaller children, be prepared to guide their thinking with practical suggestions. For example, *God stirs* the interest of their teachers and principal to help them understand the consequences of the use of drugs.

Now one final example. If you are studying the story of *Daniel in the den of the lions* (Dan. 6:1-23), who are the lions in the lives of your students, or in your community and the world? How does your parish tame them and shut their mouths for the sake of justice and peace?

LEARN TO SING A HYMN

Organists and choir directors often are a little used resource in the Sunday morning classroom. Yet many would like to be asked to occasionally assist you with your teaching.

Pick a hymn that illustrates the Bible story you have chosen, and next ask your organist to show you how to use a remarkable resource called the Hymnal Companion. Most every denomination has a Hymnal Companion, a book that gives a brief history about every hymn, when they were written, by whom and for what reason, and where the tune originated. The Episcopal Church presently uses a Hymnal Companion for the Hymnal 1940, and a new edition for the Hymnal 1982 should be in the bookstore by 1990.

But don't stop with simply selecting a hymn. Learn how to sing it, and think about introducing it to the congregation. Or consider this idea; write a new verse for the hymn that takes its cue from the Bible story you are studying, and include this new verse when you and your class sing it. Don't worry about words not rhyming. The point is, have fun. God will meet you and your students in this activity, and they will remember it long after the task is done.

Musicians can also help you present your hymn in several ways, for example, by singing its harmony or helping your class learn to sing it as a round.

Your organist would probably be more than happy to show your children how the organ itself plays. With just this kind of encouragement, your children might begin to dream about someday becoming members of the choir. That will warm any organist's heart.

Or your organist may be able to identify instrumentalists in the congregation, folks able to demonstrate their talents for the sake of your children's interest. Some may be even skilled enough to help you with hand-bells (you can even make your own) or help you play simple instruments like the recorder or cymbal.[1]

DAYS OF INTERGENERATIONAL ACTIVITY AND CELEBRATION

Days of intergenerational or interage education are appropriately included in any nine-month program, even in the very largest of churches. But if you are a small church and do not yet want to plan an "every Sunday" program, these days can also stand alone as occasional episodes of Christian education.

POINT. It is far better to provide a little Christian education every year, and have lots of fun with it, than to attempt a nine-month program when enthusiasm is not yet present.

A *Making a Banner Sunday* can involve your whole parish in the task of picturing a Bible story during a chosen season. Or groups of people can be designated to create banners of their own design. Just have plenty of scissors, glue, and banner material handy, along with coffee, juice, and a few pastries. You can also plan a *Making a Play Sunday*; just pick your story beforehand.

Christmas can be celebrated with a *Making Chrismons Sunday*, or a *Making Advent Wreaths Sunday*. Chrismons are simply Christmas tree ornaments, or monograms (mons) for Christ (Chris). They are generally made of white and gold materials, and may include such objects as a star or other symbols for Christ. A more complete discussion of Advent Wreaths, Chrismons and the decoration of a

Chrismon tree at Christmas is found on page 120 and 121 of *Creative Christian Education.*

The Epiphany season lends itself to a *Making Good News Pictures Of Jesus*, or *Making Good News Banners About Our Parish*, and Lent provides an excellent time to prepare for Easter with a *Making Easter Eggs and Butterflies Sunday.*

POINT. If you decide to make a banner, remember that BIG IS BETTER. Less is more when you consider the amount of material to explore over the course of a six-week term of study, but BIG IS BETTER when making a banner.

Most children do not remember their infant baptism, and the memory of adults naturally dims. An intergenerational event can happily develop a collage of family remembrances related to a long ago baptism. For single parents this can be an opportunity to combine with other parents to work together on helping groups of children recollect an important event in their lives. To be sensitive to possible pitfalls for single parents, ask for their help in designing such an event as this. Please see *Creative Christian Education* (p. 137) for more help with this idea.[2]

CREATE SEASONAL VESTMENTS

Colors give visual expression to seasonal themes, and they greatly assist classroom teaching and term-ending festivals. Here's how.

Every show-and-tell festival provides a grand opportunity for your class to vest your clergy with a stole or vestment that pictures what you have been exploring in the classroom. And while they are making the vestment or stole, your class will be learning afresh the story that it is designed to display and something about the origins of the vestment itself. Learning is fun, and treated this way Sunday morning Christian education is never forced on unwilling participants.

If you are fearful that you might not be "artistic" enough for such an endeavor as this, ask your rector to put you in touch with a parishioner who can assist. Or better, if you held a big parish wide registration in the spring or during September's start-up of the Sunday school, as described on pages 76 - 79 of *Creative Christian Education*, simply turn to those forms and find all the help you will ever need.

In Protestant denominations, including the Episcopal Church, there are no rubrics or canons governing the use of seasonal colors. It is a matter of both general and local custom, and this creates a wide-open field for Sunday morning creativity.

The use of colors in Christian worship began before historical reference to it. What we do know is that there was a sequence of colors in use in Jerusalem by the late twelfth century. Black was used at Christmas and for festivals of Mary the mother of Jesus. Blue was used for the Epiphany and Ascension, perhaps because the color of the sky suggests the universality of the good news of God's joining with us in Christ Jesus.

By the end of the twelfth century, Pope Innocent III had apparently persuaded the general church to move with the color sequence of red, white, green, and violet.

In medieval England, our forebears constructed the finest and newest of vestments for use at the great feasts. Plain or older vestments were used for the more regular worship of the "house." Sackcloth was used during Lent: colors, on other occasions.

What I find happening is this. A growing number of parishes construct bright banners, vestments, and altar hangings by giving this task to classes in the church school community. Term-ending festival worship is nicely enhanced, and tasks like these provide a splendid opportunity for intergenerational learning as young and old, singles and families gather together to share a common task, create something splendid, and prepare to participate in a festival shortly to arrive.

THE POINT IS THIS. Colors are vehicles of communication. They give seasonal expression to the faith of the church, and designing banners and hangings generates the kind of Christian fellowship that makes for splendid parish life.[3]

BUILD A BANNER/CREATE A BULLETIN BOARD

Every Bible story is bright with color and action, and creating a bulletin board to share both the story and the results of what your class is learning is an excellent Sunday morning activity. But when you plan the display, don't forget to show God's action. Identifying God's action makes all Christian education great.

Building a banner also provides an activity that helps God meet us through stories in the Bible. It, too, is learning at its best. Here's why.

1. The task of developing a display means the story has to be known. God uses work like this to write in our minds, from the

earliest age, recollections of his mighty acts accomplished before we were born.

2. Fellowship takes shape as the banner is made. Curiosity and imagination make the classroom a happy and joy-filled place. Communion develops, not the around-the-altar kind, but godly communion nevertheless.

3. When banners and bulletin boards are displayed, recognition and outright affection will characterize parish response. Children blossom in an atmosphere like this. And because it's God's ministry we're celebrating, parish life is considerably enhanced.

On the day of presentation, banners can be processed with the choir and clergy and recognized during announcements. Perhaps class members will offer carefully prepared explanations.

Later the banners may hang for a while in the church, or the parish hall or some other important place until their task is done. But please, once made and presented, banners ought to be displayed in the most prominent place possible. No back hall hideaway.

A teenage class once put together a magnificent collage on love, basing it on the book of Ruth and using current magazine illustrations. At other times three-dimensional presentations have been constructed.

A first grade class may wish to make individual banners the size of a sheet of writing paper because they're much easier for small people to handle.

If you decide to make a banner, remember that for most children BIG IS BETTER. Less is more when you consider the amount of material to explore over the course of a six-week term of study, but BIG IS BETTER when making a banner.

A note of caution. Please let these creations be as much the children's work as possible. There's a fine line between encouraging them to do their best, helping them develop their talents fully, and taking over the banner yourself. Sometimes the latter may be appropriate but only in the closing seconds of the eleventh hour.

In relation to the Bible story we are exploring in this activity, what visualization would you like to construct, and how would it be shown?[4]

A PLACE FOR MEMORY AND RECITATION

Memory work is appropriate for all ages, although we don't seem to value it nearly as much now as we did in the past. But I've learned to value it, and here's why.

On more than a few occasions I've stood by the bedside of those dying, offering prayer or readings from scripture as they request or as I've suggested. Many's the time I've found their lips moving along with mine as the Beatitudes were read or the Lord's Prayer shared. It seems like everyone knows "In my Father's house are many mansions" (John 14:2), and the Twenty-third Psalm. Sometimes a peaceful smile marks their lips; at other times, tears—the gentle, eye-filling kind.

Several folks later recollected all sorts of memories recalled in these moments, times early in life when they were met by God through parents, friends, and church school teachers. These were warm memories of life when it was more full than it seems now, but life held even yet, like then, in the everlasting arms of One always with us (Deuteronomy 33:27).

We owe it to our children to offer this kind of preparation for their future. I have worked with a congregation during the season of Lent learning together the Twenty-third Psalm, and I've had people thank me for it. At times like those the community of faith was joined in a common educational endeavor, and communion took shape in our midst.

And I'm not suggesting memory work as busy work. Nor memory work ever pushed as a task to be evaluated harshly. But briefly engaged, week after week, in the classroom and, indeed, in Sunday's worship, occasional memorization will, I believe, provide reference points around which we can more all the more easily be engaged by the presence of God as one known to us in our midst.

We all die. And when that hour approaches in some distant future, I hope we, too, will be able, through verse, hymn, and prayer, to join with a wider communion of saints, remembering distant times past when we were personally touched not only by others but by Another.

Include some memory work in your teaching from time to time.[5]

ADOPT A SHUT-IN

Consider adopting a shut-in for your nine month-long classroom journey. Shut-ins may never be physically present with you on Sunday morning. But you can remember them at special times of the year by sharing some of the things you're exploring in the classroom, or by showing them some of the things you've been making, like the banner, or the drama, or some specially constructed items made just for them.

It is clear, isn't it, that some of your classroom time on Sunday morning could be profitable spent working "just for them." Should you choose this ministry, your class will learn something about compassion, caring and Christian social action, and perhaps gain some further notion of reverence for a life well spent, especially as these parishioners share with the children some of their personal story and remembrances.

And by such as this, you'll be a part of the great church ministry of visitation and care. Maybe clergy can accompany you from time to time to celebrate a home communion.[6]

CELEBRATE YOUR CONGREGATION'S HISTORY

Just recently I was invited to lead a Christian education workshop at a lovely old church in a mid-western city. The church itself was replete with grand and vivid stained glass windows, and the buildings that comprised the ecclesiastical complex had been built over the course of a century. During these one hundred years, I learned, the church and the city had been closely joined by women and men who were both civic leaders and parishioners.

But when I asked the Sunday morning adult class of some 70 people about the contributions that St. Mark's had made over the course of the previous century, no one could answer. In fact, only one was able to name the date of St. Mark's founding! Many of us are naive in the extreme when our congregation's history is considered.

POINT. The more a congregation loses a knowledge of its past, the more it loses contact with its roots and heritage. Indeed, more than a few congregations flounder because there is little corporate knowledge about who they are, where they have come from and where they are going. Old timers miss being valued and newcomers haven't the slightest idea that before yesterday there was anything. There is a better way.

Certainly a consideration of congregational history ought to be a part of every newcomer and/or confirmation class, and because an exploration like this is so much fun, it could be constructed as a parish activity for a term of study and updated every few years. Epiphany's theme of light for the world is a perfect place for such

9. Church celebrates its history: a homecoming

8—The Morning Record and Journal, Meriden, Ct., Wednesday, November 30, 1977

Church goes home for St. Andrew's day

People/Perspectives

Andrews Homestead

St. Andrew's tower

BY THOMAS C. JACKSON

A city church is "going home" tonight.

Back to the colonial farmhouse where the parish began amidst the turbulence and religious intolerance of America's revolution.

Back to the Moses Andrews Homestead, an 18th century structure sandwiched between a west side hamburger stand and a city school yard.

Back to the rooms and halls where Meriden's first Episcopal service was held more than 200 years ago.

Members and friends of St. Andrew's Episcopal Church plan to gather in the homestead at 7:30 for a celebration of the congregation's history. The special service falls on the day set aside to honor the parish's patron saint, St. Andrew.

Now the home of the Meriden Historical Society, the Andrews Homestead holds a museum of local lore. In this restored 18th century structure is chronicled this community's growth from a rural farming village into an urban industrial center.

Built by Samuel Andrews III, the homestead stands at what is now the intersection of West Main Street and Chamberlain Highway. Before the Revolutionary War began, Moses Andrews — one of Samuel's sons — began to work the farm.

Moses, and much of the Andrews family, converted to the Episcopal faith before the colonies split with Great Britain. The family's step, however, was to split them from most members of their community who attended a Puritan meetinghouse on Meetinghouse Hill.

As members of the "Church of England," the Andrews family became objects of suspicion as conflict between the English King and American colonies increased.

"Though Moses Andrews was a man remarkable for his mildness and the gentleness of his character, he was placed under heavy bonds and forbidden to leave his farm under any pretense whatever, without the special permission of the local Committee of Inspection," a St. Andrew's parish history published in 1940 states.

"To Mr. Andrews, the severest part of this punishment was being forbidden to worship God with his brethren on the Lord's Day in the Lord's House of his choice," the parish history continues. "He had petitioned for permission to go to church on Sundays in Wallingford.

"This indulgence was refused him and he was graciously given leave to attend the Congregational meetinghouse in Meriden," the history continues.

Instead, Moses Andrews decided to hold his own Episcopal services.

"So he brought slabs and blocks of wood from the neighboring sawmill for benches and invited his neighbors and other friends to attend," the parish history states. "Every Sunday the small congregation, not more than 15 or 20 in all, assembled to unite in worship according to the forms of the Prayer Book and to listen to a sermon from some more or less noted divine's published works.

"Moses Andrews was usually a lay reader. For about a quarter of a century these simple services were kept up," the history states.

An administrative structure for the Episcopal Church in Connecticut was established in 1784 with the consecration of a bishop for the new diocese. This act opened the door for formal organization of a new parish in Meriden.

During 1789, a dozen men took the first step toward establishing St. Andrew's as a permanent parish. Formal organization of the congregation occurred Dec. 2x, some 17 years before Meriden and Wallingford were split into two separate communities.

The parish struggled along until another revolution swept through Meriden. The advent of an industrial age brought new life to this community. In the decade from 1840 to 1850, the town's population almost doubled as this village became a manufacturing center; a "Silver City."

St. Andrew's prospered with Industrial Revolution, finally moving to the third and present church building at the corner of East Main and Liberty Streets near city hall. Erected between 1866 and 1867, the Portland brownstone structure is a clear example of a neo-gothic architectural style.

Tonight's St. Andrew's celebration is scheduled to begin promptly at 7:30 in the Moses Andrews Homestead at 424 W. Main St. The service is set to include an informal eucharist, some old hymns and then a chance to look about the Meriden Historical Society's current home.

For St. Andrew's, the restored 18th century farmhouse will also always be home.

an exploration, and this investigation is noted in the chapter describing the Epiphany term.

To conduct such a study, interview older parishioners about the way things were and what they remember about days gone by in your church. Also pay careful attention to the way in which your congregation ministered to your city or community. Collect photographs and make a collage, or a slide presentation, or a scrapbook or a video about what you find. While you are making any of these items, search your congregation for artists who might help you make such a show as "professional" as possible. Maybe the show could include music in the background, and maybe it could be used in the future to introduce new members to your rich heritage.

As a result, you will no longer be a people without roots.[7]

SUPPORTING PARISH AND FAMILY LIFE WITH ACTIVITY

Intergenerational activity helps families enjoy tasks together on Sunday morning, and every opportunity should be made to include some interage affairs in every yearly program. But still more action commends itself.

Families can bake bread for the weekly eucharist, and recipes are readily available to make bread that does not easily crumble. Also, families can be responsible for ushering on Sunday morning, or gathering the offering when it is presented.

Family prayer is also an important interest for many Christians, but there are only so many hours in any one day, particularly in this day and age. A method of family prayer that takes into account busy schedules is found on page 73 of *Creative Christian Education.*

Activities like these strengthen family solidarity. I hope you will think about including them in your Sunday school plans.

CHRISTMAS/EASTER ACTIVITIES

A Jesse tree can be constructed at Christmas time, and along with the construction of Advent wreaths and Chrismons, all provide excellent opportunities for intergenerational education.

The idea of a Jesse tree takes its cue from Isaiah 11:1;

> There shall come forth a shoot from the stump of Jesse, and a branch shall grow out of his roots.

And the Spirit of the Lord shall rest upon him, the spirit of wisdom
and understanding, the spirit of counsel and might, the spirit of knowledge
and the love of the Lord.
And his delight shall be in the love of the Lord. (RSV)

Jesse was a direct forebear of Jesus, and Isaiah is simply saying
that "one day the stock of Jesse will come to full flower, and God
will deliver not only Israel but all of the world." To show the full
flower of this righteous branch, it might be decorated with Chrismons
or other brightly colored materials to show the fulfillment. Of course
the branch represents Jesus.

At Easter, the same branch used for the Jesse tree at Christmas
can be decorated with brightly colored Easter eggs or especially made
butterflies, so symbolizing the resurrection.

Question: How large will this branch be and where will it be
placed? Will it be a small stick of a thing tucked away in the corner
of the church, or will it be a limb worthy of the Sovereign of the
universe and sized to match. And what about the size of the butterflies
and their colors? Big and bright are always better than small and
drab in Sunday morning Christian education, for "big and bright"
will be remembered long after the day is gone.

Intergenerational activity should always include refreshments,
and several families or classes can choose to be responsible for such.[8]

Notes

1. From Howard Hanchey, Creative Christian Education
(Wilton, CT: Morehouse-Barlow, 1986), pp. 109, 126, 142.

2. Ibid., pp. 55, 92, 122.

3. Ibid., p. 20.

4. Ibid. See also the following pages for ideas to encourage your
creativity on banner making: pp. 55, 60, 83, 106, 130, 180; and on
bulletin boards: pp. 18-19, 108-9, 124-25, 143, 164-65, 171.

5. Ibid., p. 55.

6. Ibid., p. 105.

7. Ibid., pp. 135-36, 138.

8. Ibid. For Advent wreaths see p. 120; for butterflies see pp.
32, 121, 153, 163-64; for Chrismons see pp. 81, 92, 121; for Easter
egg trees see p. 163.

CHAPTER EIGHT

Gospel Drama: Old Stories with a New Twist

Teen and adult Christians want to know more about God, not less, and not simply abstract ideas about God, but the difference we can expect God to make in our daily lives.

While this chapter does not provide direct teaching assistance for those who work with children below the age of adolescence, the concepts and ideas which follow will help you become more comfortable with handling stories from the Bible, and more confident in your analysis of God's action.

But for teachers of teenagers and adults, the thoughts and concepts in this and the next chapter, along with the discussion of faith developed in chapter 3, can set you free to explore theology in ways about which you may have only dreamed in the past. Moreover, chapter 4 in *CEME* also provides you with perspectives about what this age group hopes for in Sunday morning Christian education, and some of the best ways to meet their expectations when you plan your teaching.

POINT. As we grow to adulthood, all of us wrestle more and more with the question of *why bad things happen if God is so loving and all powerful*. The theological discussion in this chapter and the next are designed to help you answer this important question, and enable the discussion of this same wonder in either your Sunday morning class or your meetings with teenagers and/or adults during the week.

ASSERTING GOD'S PRESENCE

God acts in the here-and-now of everyday life. This chapter shows how gospel drama makes just this point by working with the story of David meeting Goliath (I Samuel 17), a story cited also in chapters 6 and 7.

Now you will want to explore far more than David and Goliath in your Sunday morning teaching, so treat the use of this story as simply the illustration it is meant to be. A list of the images and metaphors I use to assert God's presence is found at the end of this and the next chapter, and each one works to help you to both explore and speculate about God's action in any Bible story you choose. So when you plan to work with any Bible story on Sunday morning, simply

—take a look at the lists of metaphors and images found at the end of this and the next chapter,
—reacquaint yourself (if necessary) with their perspectives, and
—with your students apply them to the Bible story you are exploring.

The older we grow the more we are confronted with ambiguity in life. Increasingly we learn that good does not always (or often, it sometimes seems) triumph. All of us are abused by life, and we abuse one another. Paul puts it this way: "That which I would do, I do not, and that which I would not do, I do." Adults and teens wonder why this happens and reach for understanding, not content to say that bad things are "God's will," as if God is an abusive parent. As a result of studies like these, believers will develop from infant baptized Christians, natural faith will begin to become Christian faith (chapter 3), and adults and teenagers will find their faith in God strengthened.

Gospel drama may take only a few minutes to construct, but the discussion it generates makes this a joyful method of theological education. The bulk of this chapter is devoted to a few brief pictures of God upon which gospel drama draws.

POINT: The more you know about who God is and how God meets us in the here-and-now of everyday life, the more able you will be in your teaching about God's action in the midst of life.

GOSPEL DRAMA: EASY AND FUN

Gospel drama treats every Bible story as a potential play, and it includes God and the Adversary of Scripture as active participants. Gospel drama knows that God is as close as breath to lungs and reminds us again and again that God cares, God is not distant from us, and we are never alone.

This is the way gospel drama works; it searches every Bible story for decision points, decisions that pushed events to go one way and not another, and then these decision points are explored from the perspective of God's action. To make sure this happens:

—God is introduced as a specific participant in every story (Prayer Book, p. 858, "grace"),
—human freedom and our capacity to make decisions is acknowledged (Prayer Book, p. 845, "human freedom"),
—sin is described, not as a theory, but as an always present and easily understood reality, (Prayer Book, p. 848, "sin and redemption"), and
—the Bible's Adversary of Scripture is included (Prayer Book, p. 302, the renunciations in the baptismal liturgy).

Each of these perspectives is noted in the Book of Common Prayer, and their location is shown in the parentheses.

Now briefly look with me at the story of David and Goliath presented in the previous chapter.

> David was a shepherd boy who, because he was also a good musician, was appointed by King Saul as his attendant.
> Now the Philistines had collected their forces for war against the Hebrews, and one who led them was a man named Goliath. Everyday he came forward to taunt the Hebrew armies, and there was no Hebrew who would stand up against him. But David heard Goliath's taunts one day, and he was incensed. "Who is he, a Philistine, to defy the army of the living God." David's words were reported to Saul, and after a consultation, David volunteered to meet Goliath on the battlefield. (I Samuel 17)

You know well the story of this young shepherd boy with his slingshot and smooth rocks, and how he delivered the Hebrews from Goliath's threats. Where are the decision points in this story? One point stands out when David actually heard Goliath and began to form his response. Another shows when David made his decision to volunteer to stand up against this bully.

With a decision point in mind, gospel drama next asks someone to volunteer to be David, still another to take the part of Saul or Goliath (depending upon which decision point you are dramatizing), and still two others to play the part of God and that of the Adversary of Scripture. (It's often hardest to find someone to play the part of God, for we seem to much prefer playing the part of the Adversary.)

Ask these volunteers to stand in front of the class, place David and Saul or Goliath at some convenient place, and ask "God" and the Adversary to stand just behind David, one slightly to his left and the other slightly to his right.

Now have Goliath speak forcefully, and as David hears Goliath, ask either the Adversary or God to engage David in conversation. God might say something like, "I need your help," while the Adversary might say such things as, "You're going to get yourself killed," or, "Let someone else do it."

If those who are playing God or the Adversary are initially tongue-tied, ask the class to help them out with thoughts. Also make sure that God and the Adversary don't speak in sonorous tones. Encourage them to use everyday language. God meets us where we are just as we are, and often we're so accustomed to hearing God described in the highly stylized language of Scripture that it's difficult to conceive God's presence as the friend and companion that God is.

The more your class contributes to this dialogue, the more you will see God and the Adversary in debate with one another. Soon your students are likely to be involved in a heated discussion about who God is and how God is involved in all our lives. Still later, you may choose to collate these developing perspectives on newsprint or a blackboard for further discussion and consideration. Still later you may choose to make gospel drama into a play or pageant to show to the church on Sunday morning.

"But I've never heard God speak," you say. We speculate, of course, for the sake of discussion and education. But the Bible says that God is just as interested in us as God is in the sparrows of the air (Luke 12:7), and Jesus shows us the shape of God's interest to be that of a conversational presence in the world and with us everyday.

DESCRIBING GOD'S ACTION

Including God as an explicit participant distinguishes gospel drama. And when God is acknowledged as an active participant in

Bible study, Sunday morning Christian education is transformed into powerful and purposeful theological education.

"But can we get into the mind of God?" you ask. Of course we can, and the Bible gives us all kinds of assistance. Here's how.

God Walks with Us and Talks with Us

We are not alone in the world, and God is not silent. The word *conversationalist* describes God's relationship with us, and the word itself is rooted in the Latin *con* (with) and *versari* (to travel). One grand old hymn puts it this way: "He walks with me, and he talks with me. . . ." God is one who journeys with us no matter where we are, no matter who we are.

The Bible reads like a litany of God's conversational presence in the universe: Creation begins because of God's word, "Let there be. . . ."; the Exodus from Egypt is by God's decree; God kept conversational company with young Samuel (I Samuel 3:4f.); and God spoke to Elijah in a still small voice (I Kings 19:12).[1]

Jesus is, of course, God's conversational presence and ministry in the flesh. Christians know this first of all about God; if you want to know who God is, look first of all at who Jesus is. The Bible says a lot of things about God, but the perspective of God as conversationalist that Jesus clearly shows us is bell-clear all the way through.[2]

POINT FOR EDUCATION. A conversational perspective lies at the heart of gospel drama. When God is included as a participant, have God speak plainly and in the language of the day. There's no need to come up with a grave sounding voice saying, "Thus saith. . . ," whatever they are. Ask participants to speak plain words that reflect the practicality of God's everyday care for us.

"But," you say, "what if the members of my class can't agree about what God might be saying?" Expect this to happen and rejoice because there are many possibilities in most circumstances. The point of putting words in God's mouth isn't meant to result in one person's being "right" and another "wrong." But by including a discussion of God's conversation with us, a setting is cultivated wherein we can engage weighty discussion about matters that really count in the world.

The Dialogue Between Human Spirit and God's Holy Spirit

"But if God talks so much," you say, "why don't we hear God more clearly?" Your question is a good one, and a consideration of human consciousness helps explain why we don't often hear God with clarity.

Human consciousness can be described by the shape of a pyramid:

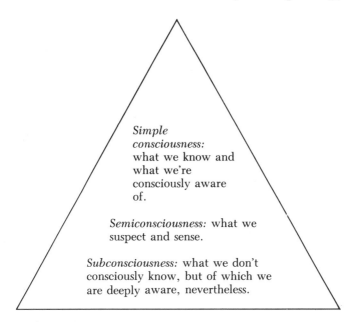

Simple consciousness: what we know and what we're consciously aware of.

Semiconsciousness: what we suspect and sense.

Subconsciousness: what we don't consciously know, but of which we are deeply aware, nevertheless.

The image of an iceberg also helps this discussion, for just as most of it lies below the surface, so too does most of us. Of course, these distinctions are artificial. But they serve to describe the complexity of our mental processes and the deeply pervasive way God is with us.

Consciousness has to do with what we know: what we see, hear, taste, feel, and understand. David was a patriot and consciously interested in the welfare of his country, so he might have leaned naturally in this direction.

But at a *subconscious* level, God was also supporting his interest. So God did what God does best: God's Holy Spirit whispered to human spirit the confirmation of an idea; courage and commitment were generated in David; and he began to make plans to go to battle.

God is always about the task of stirring us to new ideas and perspectives, even when things seem bleak and hopeless. Here is the birthplace of human hope around the world, even though the author may remain unknown.

POINT FOR EDUCATION. Gospel drama offers an opportunity to consider the way in which God touches the human psyche and speaks to the soul. So when constructing godly or adversarial dialogue, know also that what is being consciously said and heard merely signs a far more important conversation at the levels of the deep. Deep speaks to deep, and if this conversation sometimes pauses, it never quits.

God's Grace Invites Our Attention

What the church calls grace also helps explain why David responded to the need of his people. Now, a few folks might say that his response was purely one of affection or patriotism, and still others might say that it was simply good luck or good fortune. But while Christians recognize and rejoice about all the random possibilities that life generates, Christians also know more.

Consider the perspective of God's grace. Grace describes God's bottom-line attitude toward us. And just like every loving parent wants the best for their children, God wants the very best for us. The Book of Common Prayer puts it this way in response to the question, What is grace? "Grace," says the Prayer Book, "is God's favor toward us, unearned and undeserved; by grace God forgives our sins, *enlightens* our minds, *stirs* our hearts, and *strengthens* our wills." Look at the action words I've emphasized here that describe God's action, for this brief Prayer Book description accurately pictures the way the Bible shows God at work on every page of Scripture.[3]

Grace is not passive either. God did not simply look toward the plight of these Hebrews and say, "They're in trouble," or, "That's too bad." Grace played its part in this godly conversation we're considering. David felt the whisper of God's wind, and he heard a voice without words, and because of what we call grace he did not turn away. He was, of course, free to respond to God's initiative or not. But he responded positively, and that made all the difference.

POINT FOR EDUCATION. God's grace takes the shape of a stirring, idea-generating conversation in the Sunday morning classroom. So whatever the thoughts your students generate while involved in tasks like gospel drama, embrace their explorations as the godly events they are.

Your class might also enjoy a search of the Book of Common Prayer for other prayers and collects that describe God's grace, prayers that might be even more precise in their descriptions of God's action in the Bible stories you study.

DESCRIBING SIN AND THE HUMAN RESPONSE
TO GOD'S MINISTRY

If all God has to do is speak and all we have to do is act in response, God would have an easy time of it, and life would not be nearly as painful and ambiguous as it often is. But because *we aren't able to hear well* and because we are *free to listen or not,* God's ministry of care is quite difficult indeed.

Now we are brought to a second important perspective in this method of telling Bible stories: the matter of sin.

Here is what Christians call sin: we tend to listen to our own interests at the expense of God's interested-in-us conversation. Sin is fundamentally an attitude that sets our capacity to choose "our way" over the collaborative conversation to which God is always inviting us.[4]

The author of Genesis describes sin this way:

> The Lord God took Adam and put him in the garden of Eden to till and keep it. And the Lord God commanded Adam, saying, "You may eat of every tree in the garden; but of the tree of the knowledge of good and evil you shall not eat, for on the day that you eat of it you shall die." (Gen. 2:15-17, RSV)

And still later:

> But the serpent said to the woman, "You will not die. For God knows that when you eat of it your eyes will be opened, and you will be like God, knowing good and evil." So when the woman saw that the tree was good for food, and that the tree was to be desired to make one wise, she took of its fruit and ate; and she also gave some to her husband, and he ate. (Gen. 3:4-6, RSV)

God had previously told both Eve and Adam to ignore the fruit of this tree. But now another, who also seemed to have their best interests at heart, was saying, "It's really OK." Who was Eve to believe?

Even though the author of this section of Genesis does not include this particular conversation, we can be sure that God was not silent nor passive while this event was evolving. But still Eve and Adam listened to what they thought were their best interests, and they broke trust with God.

Sin is not nearly so much an action as it is an attitude. Sin might be "drinking" to some or a "cuss" word for others. Or sin might be treating God's children, our sisters and brothers, in a shabby fashion. But as destructive as our actions might be, they would not take place if we were 100 percent tuned in to the mind of God and in agreement with God's perspective.

God made us free, and we are free because we are made in his image and God is free. But still deeper, we are free because God wants us to return our love to him of our own accord. God does not at all want to coerce our love, as if coerced love could ever be love at all!

Our tendency toward sin is a function of our freedom. If we were not free, we would not sin. But if we were not free, we wouldn't be human, nor would we be made in the image of God.

But what about Original Sin? The concept of Original Sin is merely another way of saying that our human tendency to value ourselves more than God is larger and more pervasive than any one individual life. It is a part of our original equipment.

POINT FOR EDUCATION. Sin is a part of life, and gospel drama provides rich opportunities to explore sin as far more than simple moralisms about what is right and what is wrong. So when God speaks in the Bible story you choose to play, recognize that God's people are free to listen or not and to choose what or to whom they want to attend. Indeed, help your charges to be the sinners we are.

So what does this discussion tell us about David and the decision he made? Even though David was a patriot, he was free to listen to God's encouragement or not. God did not "make" David do what he did, for God does not push us around, and "making" David do something would have violated the freedom that sets us apart as created in the image of God. Still, God did stir, David was faithful, and an idea took shape.

Freedom in the Universe

Human freedom makes God's caretaking ministry difficult, for it sets us at liberty to listen first of all to ourselves and what we believe to be our best interests.

We and God have two fundamentally different perspectives on life. On the one hand we tend to play our own tune, while on the other hand God supports the welfare of all. The Bible puts it this way, "My thoughts are not your thoughts," says the Lord (Isa. 55:8). God and we don't necessarily or even often think in the same way, and the notion of freedom in the universe recognizes that in every final analysis we are free to turn from God's always interested-in-us conversation.

The psalmist also speaks of our freedom to make decisions about how we live and the way in which God sometimes chooses to deal with our selfishness.

I am the Lord your God, who brought you out of the land of Egypt and said, "Open your mouth wide, and I will fill it." And yet my people did not hear my voice, and Israel would not obey me.
So I gave them over to the stubbornness of their hearts, to follow their own devices. (Ps. 81:10-12)

A modern day story illustrates the psalmist's point.

> It is late spring, and sixteen-year-old Ashley wants a tan to enhance her white prom gown. But the date of the dance is near and there is not enough time for a leisurely schedule of sunbathing.
>
> Despite warnings from friends, the experience of others, and words of caution from the tanning industry, Ashley bathes without a sunscreen, and instead of a tan, this disappointed teen carries a bright red and painful burn to the dance.

The notion of God giving us over to the stubbornness of our hearts describes the way in which God honors our freedom.

But no matter how much we listen to ourselves, God's interested-in-us conversation never quits. So on a special day, maybe three thousand years ago, in the midst of conflicting claims upon his life and interest, David chose to draw near to the word of God. Although free, he still listened to a care-filled voice as broad as the universe, and he decided to act on the basis of what he heard.

POINT FOR EDUCATION. Such tough issues as selfishness and sin naturally come to focus when you use gospel drama. Simply discuss them briefly before the drama begins, begin the drama, and then watch them appear.

Discerning Spirit's Hope for Us: Prayer in Action

Prayer is always of interest to Christians, both children and adults, and prayer always deserves a discussion in the Sunday morning classroom.

But don't discuss prayer from esoteric or highly intellectualized perspectives. That will turn your people off. Prayer must be discussed at personal levels, and for this reason it is best likened to a conversation between a friendly God and the people God calls God's own.

Some Christians ask, "If God knows everything, why do I need to pray?" Generally these same folks think their parents ought to give them "the world" without their ever stating their needs. Still other Christians fail to distinguish between what they "need" to live and what they "want" to live, and they expect God to pay equal attention to both.

But more often than not, many Christians confuse the action of prayer with talking: we have something to say, and we expect God to listen and act in response. But far more than talking to God, prayer is listening and responding to God.

A story entitled "Coming to a Halt" illustrates.[5]

> One evening when I was complaining about a particularly tough problem in my trucking business, my sister asked, "Have you prayed about it, Bill?"
> "Sure," I quickly replied. "Whenever I can."
> "You mean 'catch as catch can,' don't you?" she said, knowing I was constantly on the run between work and home and any number of other things.
> "The Lord can hear me just as well when I'm running," I answered.
> "Yes," she said, "but can you hear Him?"

Harried lives breed anxiety, and more than anything else, anxiety gets in the way of a listening prayer. We kick and flail away, and the more we work at prayer, the less satisfied we become.

Still, Jesus assures us that "the kingdom of heaven is at hand." And he says that to take advantage of it, simply "come to me, all you who labor and are heavy laden, and I will give you rest." Prayer means a surrender of our interests and a focus on listening to God: not only to what God wants from us and for us but what God is already doing in our behalf to bring those things about.

Maybe on occasion you've found yourself so confused that you simply did not know what to do. At times of stress we're overwhelmed by an abundance of input, much like the trucking executive in the story above. But Jesus offers a guide for prayer at times like these: He drew apart for quiet and reflective meditation, to take advantage of listening to One who knew far better than he the ways and means of dealing with whatever current trauma engaged his heart.

The dialogue characterizing gospel drama is another way to consider prayer, and the dialogue itself shows why it is often so hard for Christians to determine what God might be saying. The fact is, when we pray there are at least three of us involved: God, the "forces of evil that seek to destroy life," and ourselves, with all of the wishes, fears, and desires that we bring to the moment. I hope you'll explore prayer from these perspectives with both children and adults, for it is a far better exploration of prayer than we most times engage.[6]

It *is* hard work for human beings to hear God, but harder still I suspect for God to get through to our rational consciousness, a point accurately focused each time gospel drama is used.

If you are interested in considering a study of prayer, no matter how brief, use gospel drama as the launching device. You will never lack for lively, engaged discussion.

DEALING WITH THE POWERS OF DARKNESS

If you think this section will simply say that "the devil makes us do it," you are wrong. We human beings are responsible for our actions, and the Bible makes this clear on every page. But the Bible also personifies evil to help us deal with it, and education about evil is best when we make the study of evil as personal as possible.

This is the way the Bible treats evil: In the same way that God is near and conversationally present with us, so too is evil, and there's no better illustration than the temptations of Jesus in the early pages of Matthew's Gospel.

Evil in the universe is real, personal, and far larger than any one of us or any group of us. Some of us felt this evil when, in the civil rights struggles of the sixties, clubs and guns were used by the vicious on the innocent. Others of us felt evil in Nazi Germany as Hitler rose to power. And still more of us saw it in the pictures of empty ovens at death camps like Buchenwald. Jesus himself engaged a demonic spirit, and stories of a demonic ministry are spread all through the pages of Scripture.[7]

It is difficult to engage the idea of evil in the classroom. Even at best the discussion tends to be abstract and not immediately focused. But because evil is so closely allied with our self-centeredness, it is easy to personify. By placing an Adversary in every Bible play, we are enabled to deal with evil in a nonthreatening fashion.

POINT. I prefer to use the term *Adversary of Scripture* instead of *Satan* or *the devil,* mainly because I don't want to confuse the Bible's perspective with shabby cult practices or accounts of demon possessions.

If at all possible, add a part for the Adversary of Scripture whenever you dramatize a Bible story. The Adversary helps us discuss the nature of evil, not as an abstract concept, but as something that touches us where we live. If a loving God stands at the door of our lives and knocks (as the author of Rev. 3:20 puts it) and tugs for a hearing, the Bible says that so does another. But most of all, the concept of the Adversary is a foil that helps us all the more value God's ministry and the way we stand in need of it.

Although the Bible makes no mention of the Adversary in the story of David and Goliath, we can bet the Adversary was present. For just as God seeks our companionship, so does the Adversary of Scripture. But while God offers us bread to eat and always seeks to stir us to better things, the Adversary plays upon our natural tendency to listen to ourselves (I Pet. 5:8).

So what can we say of the Adversary's interest that afternoon almost three thousand years ago? The Adversary might have encouraged David to consider his own welfare and safety, and had David leaned toward this conversation, he would probably have remained safely at home.

Most every Bible story makes it possible to cite the ministry of the Adversary of Scripture, and by including it when you forge gospel drama, you give every participant an excellent opportunity to begin discussions about why bad things happen in God's world if God is so good.

POINT FOR EDUCATION. There is a streak of meanness in most every one of us, but the Bible says there's more. Adding the Adversary to Bible stories when they are played introduces a note of the evil that is never far from us and makes for lively discussion about matters that really count. I don't add an Adversary to stories when working with preschool through fourth-grade children. But by the time of the fifth and sixth grades, children are able to enjoy using this addition without becoming scared by it.

God Deals with Our Selfishness

Our lives provide a rich playground for the Adversary of Scripture, and the word *selfishness* defines what results. The word itself describes our original equipment tendency to make sure that our personal interests are served first of all. This tendency is naturally derived, for to survive in the early years of Creation we had to look out first of all for ourselves. Darwin was right: Adaptability bred us for life, and the demand to adapt requires that we look out, first of all, for what we think are our own best interests.

But God's grace abounds even in the midst of selfishness. God does not desert us. Even if David, like us, was subject to selfishness, he was also in communion with God. And because God's interested-in-us conversation never quits, as a result of grace David put aside personal self-interest and risked his life for others.

Working with the subject of selfishness also provides a rich opportunity to distinguish between appropriate self-interest and selfishness. Developing healthy self-esteem in young people is an important task, and self-esteem is rooted in an appropriate use of self-interest. It is not selfish to study to meet the requirements for a school test. This is appropriate self-interest. But it is selfish to remove a book from the library so that others cannot prepare. It's also stealing.

POINT FOR EDUCATION. As you construct God's conversation in gospel drama, shape the conversation so that God is always offering a better idea, and always encourage those who take the part of the Adversary to play to the selfish side of things. Highlight this theme by asking questions like, "What signs of selfishness can we see in this story?" or, "How would you struggle with selfishness if you were in this story?"

Just as the voice of a master tuning fork elicits sympathetic vibrations from other forks nearby, because of God's interest all of us resonate to possibilities larger than we have any reason to expect.

God's Love and God's Powerlessness

Tens of thousands of people are killed every year on America's highways. Is God not interested? The bottom line is this: Freedom means that we can drive as we please (even if the law says otherwise). Although God provides a cautionary word when necessary and even harsh judgment when warranted, we are free to choose to abuse the rules of the road. In the final analysis we are always free to listen to God, or not.

The notion of the powerlessness of God walks hand in hand with the matters of sin and freedom, and we don't pay enough attention to either in Christian education. That's why many people are hungry to read any book written about why bad things happen to us.

The idea of God's powerlessness is perhaps one of the thorniest issues Christians are expected to address. In part our difficulty stems from highly idealized pictures of an all powerful God generated, at least in part, by early childhood pictures of our parents. For most of us these were people who solved sticky problems and made every-thing all right, even when things were not right. They were all powerful and all knowing, a point expanded in the next chapter. And still others of us, because we were subject to harsh parental abuse or neglect during our formative years, have all kinds of trouble coming to believe in a God of solicitous affection.

But Christians who have the most trouble with the notion of God's powerlessness are those who have not taken the time to consider the value God places on human freedom, nor the pervasive way in which what theology calls "sin" compromises life. Nor do these folks give much of a consideration to what the Prayer Book calls "those forces of evil which seek to destroy life."

You may not agree with all that is in this section's brief discussion, but if you do not, take it up with the Bible's witness, and if you are an Episcopalian, with the thoughts contained in the Prayer Book.

These books of faith are the benchmarks against which many of us measure our thinking about the things of God.

The Bible itself contributes to the overblown power perspectives we attribute to God by generating its own highly idealized picture of God's ruling might, a picture which the Jesus who suffers in the hands of the world seeks to modify.

The fact is, the range of God's ministry is far broader than our human ability to describe it adequately. God has been traditionally described as

—omnipotent—all powerful,
—omniscient—all knowing,
—omnipresent—everywhere, and
—infinite—always and forever.

Although these descriptions point toward the truth of who God is, in and of themselves they do not adequately portray the range of God's love in the midst of human life. In fact, the first three attributes better describe a steely-eyed cowboy from the old west than they portray the biblical ministry of one who serves and consents to die on a cross. And each of these ideas pays too little attention to the human freedom God bestows on us, and for God the consequences of our freedom.

Describing God's presence and ministry in the midst of life means using paradox, and paradox is precisely what these three attributes leave out.

Dietrich Bonhoeffer, in the midst of Hitler's terrible exercise of freedom and power, struggled to make sense of God's providence, human freedom, and the holocaust taking place all around him. Well over 30 million human beings lost their lives during this period of world history, and the question asserted itself for Bonhoeffer just like it does for us, "If God is so good, why do things get so much out of hand?"

Bonhoeffer was a German national and budding theologian of world repute who, while on a lecture tour in the United States in 1939, was urged by his friends to stay in safety. But he decided instead to return to Germany, taking one of the last ships to leave for his homeland before the war began.[8]

Later Bonhoeffer unsuccessfully plotted with a group of fellow citizens to kill Hitler, he was subsequently arrested on April 5, 1943, imprisoned, and on the gray dawn of Monday, April 9, 1945, Bonhoeffer was executed in Flossenburg, Germany. The camp doctor saw Bonhoeffer kneeling in preparation and praying fervently, and the prayer on his lips may have been much like one he wrote late in the summer of 1944.[9]

> God, who dost punish sin and willingly forgive, I have loved this people. That I have borne its shame and burdens, and seen its salvation— that is enough. Seize me and hold me! My staff is sinking; O faithful God, prepare my grave. (From *Der Tod des Mose*, written by Dietrich Bonhoeffer in the late summer of 1944 [Lettner Verlag].)[10]

Before death, Bonhoeffer spent his two years of imprisonment corresponding with a few close friends and the members of his family. He also spent a lot of time considering the reason why terrible things were occurring all around him. Eventually he came to a place of pondering what he called the powerlessness of God.

Alone now in his cell, positioned in the center of the world's devastation, parted forever from friends and family and yet, still knowing the company of God, Bonhoeffer writes:

> Before God and with God we live without God. God lets himself be pushed out of the world on to the cross. He is weak and powerless in the world, and that is precisely the way, the only way, in which he is with us and helps us. Matt. 8:17 makes it quite clear that Christ helps us, not by his omnipotence, but by virtue of his weakness and suffering.
>
> Here is the decisive difference between Christianity and all religions. Man's religiosity makes him look in his distress to the power of God in the world: God is the *deus ex machina* [Author's note: a description of the practice in classical tragedies of introducing god to solve abruptly a difficulty or problem] [But] . . . the Bible directs man to God's powerlessness and suffering; only the suffering God can help. [This] . . . opens up a way of seeing the God of the Bible, who wins power and space in the world by his weakness.[11]

Above all else the notion of God's powerlessness asserts that God is a servant, just as Paul notes in the brief hymn he includes in his letter to the Christians at Philippi (Phil. 2: 5-11), One who respects human freedom, denies not the reality of sin and likes it not one bit, but One who for the sake of love consents to serve us as a people chosen forever.[12]

The powerlessness of God is not a new motif in Christian thought. It begins with Adam and Eve and the serpent in the very first chapter of Genesis, it continues all though the Bible to reach a crescendo at Calvary with its cross, and it is indirectly noted in several collects in the Book of Common Prayer.

> We remember this day, O God, *the slaughter of the holy innocents of Bethlehem by the order of King Herod.* Receive, we beseech thee, into the arms of your mercy all innocent victims; and by thy great might frustrate the designs of evil tyrants and establish thy rule of justice, love, and peace . . . . (Book of Common Prayer, p. 238)

God did not want these youngsters destroyed. But because Herod feared that another might take his place, to be sure of Jesus' death he murdered all the children in the neighborhood (Matt. 2:16-18). Herod was free to act as he chose, and in that moment God was powerless.

God has a tough row to hoe in the midst of our lives. A sovereign God will not abuse us like abusive parents coerce their children, and God does not twist our arms until we cry "uncle." Rather, God depends upon the irresistible grace of his conversational presence with us.

Now return with me to the story of David and Goliath. Had David turned from the godly conversation, God would have been powerless with him in that moment. God then would have looked someplace else for help, if God had not already begun to do so.

POINT FOR EDUCATION. Gospel drama offers grand opportunities to wrestle with the breadth of God's ministry in the world. It also helps underscore the fact that we human beings are largely responsible for what is wrong in the world, and it encourages us to begin to think about more responsible patterns of living. So when, in this method of telling Bible stories, the part of God converses with the human participants, watch out for signs of sin, selfishness, and the powerlessness of God. But also watch for the pervasive power of grace, which often proves irresistible.

In any final analysis, the notion of God's powerlessness always warns Christians to beware of the strength of our freedom and our abuse of it. And you need look no further for the way in which this concept serves to alert us than to consider what we are doing to the world's natural resources, particularly to the air we breathe. Will we reach a point in the destruction of our resources from which there will be no turning back? Will God, indeed *can* God intervene to prevent our destruction and, if God can, what will be the shape of this intervention? Moreover, if God is not a *deus ex machina*, then how can God act in our behalf? Here are worthy topics for both teen and adult discussion.

SECURING WHAT WE LEARN

I hope by now that you can see why I so much enjoy an occasional and spontaneous use of gospel drama. It is fun to use. Making Bible stories into plays is good teaching, and when we tell stories of God's mighty acts in the past, God stirs us to the truth of his loving care in our lives today. As a result, Christian faith becomes stronger.

The following list catalogs the images and metaphors used in this chapter. They can of course be used when discussing any Bible story. But when you use any story of any kind, look first for *turning points*, and then consider the shape of God's action in response to human need and the opportunity presented for ministry.

—God walks with us and talks with us.
—The dialogue between human spirit and God's Holy Spirit.
—The shape of human consciousness and the godly conversation.
—God's grace invites our attention.
—Sin in response to God's ministry.
—Freedom in the universe.
—Discerning the Spirit's hope for us: Prayer in action.
—The powers of darkness.
—Human selfishness.
—God's love and God's powerlessness.

As your discussion draws to a close, think to ask two questions like these to secure the learning:

What did you learn about God in this discussion?
What did you learn about yourself?

The whole point of Bible study is to learn more about God's action in the midst of life—not abstract ideas about God, but ideas about the shape of his care in the here-and-now of everyday life. Bible stories are an indispensable resource in this task because they have the power to convince an unbelieving world of the richness of love right before our eyes.

So choose Bible stories, a couple every year. Play them, discuss them, and watch God use them to bond your class more closely to the Sovereign's love.

Then watch Sunday morning Christian education become the kind of powerful theological education that builds up God's church.

Notes

1. Walter Brueggemann, "Covenanting as Human Vocation," *Interpretation, A Journal of Bible and Theology 33* (April 1970): 118. Perhaps too demanding for those unfamiliar with academic theology, Brueggemann's summary of God's conversational presence in the Bible is excellent and brief.

2. The Book of Common Prayer, on God the Son, p. 849.

3. The Book of Common Prayer, on grace, p. 858.

4. The Book of Common Prayer, on human nature, p. 845.

5. Bill Watkins, "Coming to a Halt," *Guideposts* (August 1988): p. 13.

6. The renunciations in the baptismal liturgy (the Book of Common Prayer, p. 302) speak of those forces that seek to destroy life.

7. The ministry of the Adversary of Scripture, one who tempted Jesus in the wilderness (Matt. 4:1-11), is described briefly in the renunciations of the Prayer Book's Baptismal Office, p. 302.

8. Dietrich Bonhoeffer, *Letters and Papers from Prison,* edited by Eberhard Bethge (London, SCM Press, 1967), p. 21.

9. Ibid., p. 234.

10. Ibid., p. 234.

11. Ibid., p. 196.

12. For additional readings on the powerlessness of God, see Howard Hanchey, *Creative Christian Education* (Wilton, CT: Morehouse-Barlow, 1986), pp. 157-63. Also see Thomas C. Oden, *Pastoral Theology, Essentials in Ministry* (San Francisco: Harper and Row, 1983), pp. 223-48, a brief and thoughtful discussion of the relationship between God's power, God's powerlessness—or self-limitation—and human freedom, written from the perspectives of pastoral care.

CHAPTER NINE

Learning to Speak of God in Today's World: Helping Christians Grow in Faith

Above all else, mission-minded Christian educators enjoy studies about God and God's ministry in the world. Hence, Bible study for mission-minded Christians is an important event. But these same Christians also know that God is just as much present in the here-and-now of life today, and that signs of God's ministry and action are today just as much evident to eyes of faith. But the problem is this; we need to develop these "eyes" to see God more clearly.

This chapter uses the tools developed in the preceding three chapters to explore God's action in four "canned" stories set in the here-and-now of life today. They are presented as guides to help you see how easy it is to address wonders like, "If God is so good why do bad things happen to us?" As a result of studies like these, believers will develop from infant baptized Christians, natural faith will become Christian faith, and adults will find their faith in God strenghtened.

Now you will want to explore with your students far more than the four stories presented in this chapter. But these stories serve best by helping you see how easy this task can be. They also serve to encourage you to identify personal stories from your own and your student's every day life, or even stories from the daily newspaper or monthly magazines. God is present in the here-and-now of everyday life, and with just a few faith perspectives, every story is an open window to the universe of God's presence and ministry. So treat these stories as the illustrations they are meant to be.

A list of the Bible and Prayer Book images and metaphors I use to assert God's presence in the here-and-now of life today is found at the end of this chapter, and it includes the images and metaphors used in the last chapter. Each one is designed to help you both explore and speculate about God's action in any life story you choose. So when you plan to work with life stories, simply

—take a look at the lists of metaphors and images found at the end of this and the preceding chapter,
—reacquaint yourself (if necessary) with their perspectives, and
—with your students apply them to the life story you and they are exploring.

But here's part of what we are toiling against: Every year I work with a small group of senior seminarians, soon to be ordained clergy, exploring the art of their preaching. And every year I'm also surprised to find that after two years of academic theological education, these soon-to-be ordained clergy struggle, many mightily, to speak plainly of God's action in both their sermons and everyday discourse. Although they use in their first year Old Testament course a book by G. Ernest Wright entitled *God Who Acts*, by their senior year they are still unable to speak with easy clarity or confidently declare God's action in the here-and-now of life today. Their thoughts are, for the most part, highly intellectualized concepts or philosophical speculations. I also know this sad fact, that whenever clergy cannot easily speak of God their congregations will follow suit.

As noted in chapters 1 and 3, mission-minded congregations and their clergy enjoy a different approach to the celebration of God's ministry, and their Sunday school programs reflect it. They know God is an everyday presence in the here-and-now of life today, they know that "the kingdom of heaven is at hand . . . ," and they enjoy celebrating God's everyday action in their midst. They enjoy speaking plainly of God, and they don't feel much threatened when different perspectives surface. These Christians know that God's love is rich and multifaceted, meeting us just as we are, where we are. And they enjoy identifying and announcing this Sovereign's ministry in plain, everyday language.

People in the church and in the world plainly hunger to hear of the things of God in ways that make a difference in their lives. The Bible is written from this perspective, and this chapter is designed to offer you an opportunity to develop this same atmosphere in your Sunday morning program. Simply look for signs that "the kingdom of heaven is at hand . . ." in each of the four stories. Next, take everyday stories from your life and the life of your congregation. And then, in them celebrate God's action using the same perspectives.

RENEWING OUR PICTURES OF GOD

Everyone of us has a complex (and unique) picture of God, and it formed over the course a lifetime. Some of our most vivid images are rooted in childhood, while others were formed during adolescence. Still later, adult images of God took shape as we redrew earlier pictures because of more recent experiences.

Paul puts it this way:

> When I was a child, I spoke like a child, I reasoned like a child, I thought like a child: and when I grew up I gave up childish ways. For now we see in a mirror dimly . . . .(I Cor. 13:11-12a)

All of us grow up with ideas about God gleaned from news magazines and papers, parents and Sunday school. But these images and pictures are both a blessing and curse. They are a blessing because they offer a means to effectively identify God's presence and see signs of his ministry in the world.

But these early formed images can also function like a curse, and here's why. Most adults who leave the community of faith leave because their knowledge of God doesn't keep pace with the reality of their lives. For example:

It is often difficult for adult or teenage friends of a person killed by a drunk driver to keep faith if their knowledge of God is no wider than a first grade Sunday school image of God as a heavenly, "always providing good things" parent. No matter how legitimate this image is, it is not an adequate picture of a God who has chosen to love a self-serving, sinful people, nor of a God who respects our freedom even when we choose to destroy one another.

Life is a journey from birth to death, and our old-time images of God and ourselves are always subject to renewal.

For example, many of us are learning today that we must be about the task of helping God take care of the world. We can't any more be profligate with our waste and pollutants. We are overwhelming our environment, and there will be no beneficent parent around to bail us out. As a result, there is a growing church-wide focus on mutual responsibility and interdependence. We are understanding sainthood in a new way. Saints are no longer folks who lived only in ages past, but people like you and me. Illustration 10 shows only a few ways that some of us are serving God today.

I hope you will expand this idea of modern day sainthood, our interdependence and our understanding of God by following the suggestion in illustration 10. Exercise your childhood curiosity about how you help God take care of the world, and make it a part of the All Saints or Epiphany terms of study. Images of God are being renewed today, as are our images of ourselves, and discussion generated by the ideas in this chapter goes a long way toward helping Christian faith mature.

THINKING ABOUT GOD AFRESH

Before adults and teens can take advantage of thinking about God afresh, already present images need to be acknowledged. So when you begin to help your class think about God's presence and ministry in the here-and-now of everyday life, first help your class distinguish between the way they thought of God at age five or six, the way they conceived of God when they were in their teens, and the way in which they know God now. If you are not sensitive to these issues of growth and maturation, you may find your students in a tug of wills about who is right and who is wrong, instead of feasting at a table rich with more delights than they or you expected before you began.

I've learned to expect the following perspectives to appear in this kind of discussion.

Reflecting back on childhood perspectives, adults often remember believing that God had a cookie-cutter law ready to apply to every human situation. God was like a parent who always knew better, one who took control of our lives, bailed us out when things looked bleak, and generally stood between us and adversity. God was

—like a grandfather or a
—Santa Claus who brought us gifts if we were good. God was
—taller than Dad; he was generally

10. Helping God Take Care of God's World: Saints of God at Work

One Saint of God helps
God's world with the
task of communication
and sharing information.

Three Saints of God,
although they wouldn't
call themselves such,
help God order the
world by keeping our
machinery working.

Suggestion:
Take photographs of
your congregation at
work helping God take
care of the world. Next,
display them. All Saints,
All Of Us.

—white,
—always had his hands and arms stretched out,
—had a halo and was bathed in light, and
—wore flowing robes. God was also
—like an Aladdin's lamp, but the genie was comforting and
    protective. God
—could do anything, and
—like our parents, was always ready to listen.

These simple images reflect parental influence; they are informed by cultural perspectives; they note mystery; and they are larger than life.

Our perspectives shift by the time we move into our teenage years, and though to some degree the perspectives of childhood carry forward, added are concerns about power, stability, and condemnation. God is

—a rule giver,
—intrusive, always everywhere,
—a judge,
—restrictive,
—a healer,
—a friend,
—a distant but loving father (or parent),
—forgiving,
—stability in the midst of instability,
—like a Greek god, one who is always testing us,
—personal,
—fair-minded,
—one who expects us to be responsible,
—big as the sky, and just about as impersonal.

Teenagers are struggling to become their own person. They want to find their place in life as a responsible adult, and their ideas about God reflect these issues.

By our adult years God is often seen as one with

—a sense of humor, one who
—feels our pain, and who
—needs us to help him take care of his world. God is
—more personal than ever, and
—like a father (or parent) who is also a friend.

There is truth in all three sets of these images, and there are no right or wrong answers.

To begin the process of renewing old images of God and developing new ideas, examine the present day experience that your students bring to Sunday morning Christian education. Both the good news method of telling Bible stories and gospel drama are designed to bring to your class stories and concerns from the here-and-now of everyday life. So when they emerge, help your students tell the story, look for turning points, and speculate about God's everyday care in the here-and-now of everyday life.

BEGIN WITH COINCIDENCE

Whenever I begin the task of identifying signs of God's presence and ministry in the midst of life, a coincidence is the first thing for which I look.

When something good happens to us, I immediately begin to look for still more signs of God's creativity at work in the world. But theological inquiry attends not only to fortunate coincidence but as well to painful and destructive coincidence. So when I see pain and destruction I don't stop making theological inquiry, I simply change my focus a bit and look for signs of the misuse of human freedom, indications of sin and what I identified in chapter 8 as God's powerlessness.

This chapter contains four stories drawn from the here-and-now of everyday life, and each story is used to illustrates a way to speak of God's action in our lives today. They are designed to guide you in picking stories to present to your Sunday school class. Or better, they may encourage you to ask members of your class to present their own stories for class exploration.

Sara's story offers the perspective of a fortunate coincidence, and that's where we will begin.

STORY 1: NOT A SPARROW FALLS

Madison Avenue is always dreaming up new invitations to help us spend our money. And so it was for Sara. She had lived with the same pair of glasses for fifteen years, and although the style was dated, they were still serviceable.

But I began to think, "It's been fifteen years. Why not?"

So Sara made an appointment with an ophthalmologist. He examined her eyes, and then introduced the drops to check for glaucoma. Everything seemed routine until, says Sara,

"He began to literally dance around the chair. He was really upset, and though I usually keep my cool, my heart beat fast as well."

"Your eye is ready to hemorrhage," he said, "and there's not a minute to lose. You can go to Johns Hopkins, but I have the equipment to carry out the necessary procedure right here." And so he did.

"If I had not gone to see him when I did, I might have lost the sight in this eye," she said, pointing to her right.

"And it would have been too late if I had waited just another month."

Now this question. Why did Sara begin to think about changing her glasses? Was it simply vanity, or was it only good luck?

Some will call it fortunate, and it was. And still others may think,

Give an infinite number of monkeys
an infinite number of typewriters, and
one of them will come up with King Lear,
one with Holy Scripture,
one with the Bible with one typo,
and on
and on
and on.

Random chance is infinitely random. And because it is, we could, like most of the world, drop our discussion at this point. But Christian theology provides thoughtful alternatives to this somewhat bleak perspective.

POINT. It seems to me that we can plainly see signs of God's grace stirring in this story. Sara's conversation with herself is an expression of a much deeper, unconscious dialogue with a loving God who has not a thing of greater interest than her welfare.

The world will not see these things that we call mysteries, but to eyes of faith events like these sing with the song of life.

LUCK OR CHANCE, OR SOMETHING MORE

"God provides" the old saying goes, and so it was for Sara. Providence is a description of God's ministry the church has valued for centuries. Though the word itself is used only once in all of Scripture (Acts 24:2), the idea is quite biblical.

The word itself combines the Latin *pro* (for and before) and *video* (seeing), suggesting God's

—capacity to see ahead of wherever we are and God's
—benevolent care providing for our welfare long before we have need or
—even know we might have need.

The pillars and fire and cloud in the Hebrew Exodus from Egypt are visual expressions of God's providence (Exod. 13:21). Though we don't see pillars of fire and cloud today, fire is a good metaphor for the godly interest that began to burn in Sara's heart and the bright fire that fanned her doctor's interest.

But even more, if you want to see God's providence, take a look at the life and ministry of Jesus. Jesus is God's providential ministry in the flesh and shows us what God's care looks like in our lives.

When people in his neighborhood were sick, Jesus was there, and whenever he could supply a need, he offered.

As well as any story, Jesus' feeding the five thousand illustrates God's providing ministry.

After an exhausting week or two, and upon hearing of the execution of his cousin, John the Baptist, Jesus withdrew to what Matthew calls a "lonely place."

But Jesus' reputation had spread, and crowds followed.

> And as Jesus went ashore he saw a great throng; and he had compassion on them, and healed their sick.
> When it was evening, the disciples came to him and said, "This is a lonely place, and the day is over; send the crowds away to go into the villages and buy food for themselves."
> Jesus said, "They need not go away; you give them something to eat."
> They said to him, "We have only five loaves here and two fish."
> And he said, "Bring them here to me." (Matt. 14:13-21)

Maybe it was because Jesus was tired that he did not notice that the crowd was hungry. But his disciples noticed, and as a result of their interest, Jesus took the five loaves and two fishes and fed a multitude.

God supplied a crowd's hunger with food when they gathered on a hillside almost two thousand years ago, God supplies our needs today, and God took care of Sara.

So we are left with something like this. Sara was stirred to make an appointment with her doctor. Maybe it was partly her vanity, and maybe it was also more. Was it simply intuition, or was it providence. . . or was it some of both? You be the judge. But the Book of Common Prayer makes this claim.

> Almighty God, the fountain of all wisdom, you know our necessities before we ask and our ignorance in asking: Have compassion on our weakness, and mercifully give us those things which for our unworthiness we dare not, and for our blindness we cannot ask. . . . (Book of Common Prayer, p. 231).
>
> Grant, O Lord, that the course of this world may be peaceably governed by your providence . . . . (Book of Common Prayer, p. 229).

All of us are prone to pray to God for help. But it continues to amaze me that, as often as we ask for it, when help does come our way, we find it hard to believe that it really is God's action in the midst of life.

So look for signs of a fortunate coincidence when you examine stories from the here-and-now of everyday life, stories that show a need being met that may have been, as it was in this story, unknown. And don't forget to say thank you.

ENCOURAGED BY ST. PAUL

St. Paul would dearly approve of this method of Christian education, mainly because he often identified God's presence and ministry, and shows it on his trip to Athens (Acts 17:16-34).

Paul was a stranger in town, and he found himself provoked that no one knew God.

But how to make an introduction? Paul could have gotten the Athenians' attention by condemning their lack of belief or by telling them they were wrong or even ignorant. But quite likely he'd have been run out of town, and he would not have gotten the hearing he wanted.

So this is what Paul did: he found an object with which the Athenians were familiar, and he began to offer sensitive interpretation about God's presence and ministry from Bible perspectives.

By the time Paul finished his preaching a few new believers had joined him, "including Dionysius, a member of the Court of Areopagus; also a woman named Damaris, and others besides."(Acts 17:34)

Bible scholars don't cite Paul's visit to Athens as much of a success when measured against the size of the churches he founded in other areas of Asia Minor. But because of his ministry some there were introduced to God, and scholars have no reason to believe that Paul did not function in this same winning way at other times.

As a result, across the centuries this story of an "Altar to an Unknown God" has intrigued generations of Christians.

The ability to identify signs of God's presence and ministry characterized Paul's ministry, and because of it the early church grew rapidly. Christian churches who exercise this ministry today are also growing rapidly.

Now there were a couple of things Paul did not do when bearing witness to God in the world, and we shouldn't do them either when we explore God's presence and ministry.

Paul did not demand that people see things his way when he introduced God to them (although his admonitions were more direct once they were in the church). Nor did he say, "I'm right," and, "you're wrong"—power was not his game.

Paul also knew full well that just to tell a person to believe in God was foolishness. Simply asking for belief without pointing out God's already present ministry is like offering a stone when what's possible is pointing out signs of the already present Bread of Life.

What Paul did best was help folks see in their lives signs of God's presence and ministry, and he prided himself on being able to talk with people in ways they could understand. He puts it this way:

> For though I am free from all, I have made myself a slave to all, that I might win the more.
> To the Jews I became a Jew, in order to win Jews; to those under the law I became as one under the law—though not being myself under the law—that I might win those under the law. . . . To the weak I became weak, that I might win the weak.

I have become all things to all people, that I might be all means save some. I do it all for the sake of the gospel, that I may share in its blessings. (I Cor. 9:19-20, 22-23)

Paul gives us more than a good hint about what makes for good adult education and preaching today, and by using stories from the here-and-now of everyday life, we can help the people of God in the same way that he did.

One Christian puts it this way.

> Finding God is not finding a Reality strange and new; it is recognizing and responding to Someone whom we have always known, although perhaps we knew it not. It is answering "Yes" to a Voice one has often heard, but to which heretofore one may not have been willing or prepared to listen.
>
> But that Voice, though it speaks in our hearts, is not our voice. It comes from heights and depths we cannot scale or fathom. And the words the Voice speaks are not ours. They are the words of the One who is as far as he is near, in whom alone our partial, thwarted lives have meaning and wholeness, and for whose sake alone even the least of these little ones has infinite worth.[1]

Using just a few images and metaphors for God, stories from everyday life offer every one of us an opportunity to see afresh the breadth of God's love and the complexity of his ministry, given human freedom.

THREE WAYS TO USE LIFE STORIES IN THE CLASSROOM

The story from Sara's life can be treated in three ways in the Sunday morning classroom, and each approach uses the principles developed in both the good news method of telling Bible stories and gospel drama:

1. *Teacher taught.* It can be presented and interpreted by the teacher and then discussed in general by the whole class.

2. *Class discussed.* It can be briefly presented to the whole class, interpreted and discussed in small groups (I've found four persons to be the best number) who later report back to the whole.

3. *Dramatized.* It can be made into a brief play (one including the human principles, God, and the Adversary of Scripture), and then discussed from the perspectives of God's presence and ministry.

If you play Sara's story as a drama, you will doubtless include an interested God making use of Sara's vanity to bring her to a place of help. You may include an Adversary suggesting that she put it off. You will see her wrestle with just what decision to make, struggling with conflicted thoughts and feelings. And you will likely find yourself wondering quite deeply why, after fifteen years, she decided to make an appointment in this crucial week.

But no matter which way you use to explore God's ministry in stories from everyday life, you will need a working knowledge of a few basic images of God like those introduced in this and the preceding chapter.

CONSTRUCTING CLASSROOM DRAMA

Drama sets imagination free to wonder and dream, and keeps classroom interest at a high level. Many of us don't have much time with which to work on Sunday morning, and an occasional dramatization provides just the right amount of spice to keep things interesting.

Now, by drama I don't mean a carefully choreographed play. I mean fun. The whole point of constructing a play is to have the participants enter into a discussion of God's ministry in the world so that they can begin to see, and seeing, begin to believe in God more deeply.

Any life event can be made into a story. Simply take an event that interests you, determine its beginning and its end, and look for turning points.

POINT. Pay careful attention to turning points, or places where a decision was made or not made. These are the places where we can imaginatively speculate about God's ministry, the dilemma faced by the human principals, and the influence of the Adversary of Scripture.

Your play will include the human characters, it will include God (probably in several different places), and it will include the Adversary of Scripture. Enjoy selecting the "cast," make up the dramatic action as you go along (it's important to "be loose" and have fun), and encourage the participants to talk about God's action and that of the Adversary as the play takes shape.

Now, because you're going to use it in a classroom setting, print the story so that a copy can be placed in everyone's hands. I have found that in this kind of study we work better when we can both hear and see the words. The printed story becomes our text.

Next, read it aloud no matter which of the three approaches you decide to use. Then, as it is discussed from the perspectives of God's care, ask questions like these about God's ministry:

—What signs of God's care can I see in this story?

—What signs of God's creativity are present?

—Where are there signs of human freedom and sin?

—Where did God try to "do right" by us, and where did we work against it?

Then ask these questions about our relationships with one another:

—Where did we go wrong?

—What signs are there of selfishness?

—Was God able to redeem selfishness and make it work for good?

—Are there any signs of God's powerlessness in the face of human freedom?

Finally, look for signs of the forces of evil that seek to destroy life, and speculate about the ministry of the Adversary of Scripture.

Each one of these questions emerges naturally when the story is made into a play. If, however, you feel a bit inadequate about creating a play, ask your class for help. Most every class of adults will have a "director" in their midst, perhaps unacknowledged.

STORY 2: MAKING OVER A TEENAGE DISAPPOINTMENT

God is never too busy to work in our behalf, and to God nothing is unimportant. This next story also begins at a point of fortunate coincidence, and still later interpretation offers three perspectives on God's ministry to us.

Stephanie didn't make the tennis team, and because of it she was going to miss being part of a team sport in her high school junior year. That was a painful thought.

Earlier in the year she had given a few moments thought to trying out for the volleyball team. But that sport had been her second choice, and now participation was no longer a possibility because the volleyball team had been chosen while the tennis team was being selected.

Stephanie was learning one of the harder lessons of life; we live and die by our decisions.

Hoping it would help and because she knew that her parents would be interested, Stephanie talked out her disappointment at Tuesday night supper. But her disappointment lingered, at least until she heard the results of what transpired at the next day's school lunch.

This is what happened. At that midday meal the volleyball coach elected to sit near Stephanie's mother, also a teacher, even though she, the coach, regularly found a seat at the other end of the cafeteria. But because she took this seat this day she overheard Stephanie's mom speak about the way her daughter was learning to accept life's inevitable disappointments.

And without knowing of Stephanie's now burning interest in volleyball, she leaned over and innocently asked her colleague if it would be appropriate to invite Stephanie to try out for the volleyball team.

They were just this day two players short; one had broken her ankle and the other had to drop off the team because her grades were low.

"Two roads diverged in a wood and I— /I took the one less traveled by," wrote poet Robert Frost, "and that has made all the difference." Why do we make the daily decisions that we make, and are we the only ones involved?

Or more, is it simply chance,

intuition,
telepathy,
good fortune,
luck,
fate,
or
God's providence?

Now each of us is free to conceive this coach's idea as generated by the needs of her team, an overheard conversation, and the work of her mind alone. Informal networking takes shape around the world all the time. And moreover, because of it, solace is often brought to disappointment and peace to troubled hearts. But according to the Bible, the gifts of solace and peace are gifts given only by God.

The fact is this; God cares for us, and God knows us well enough to number the hairs on our head (Matt. 10:30). From the earliest possible time, God had been quietly working to make Stephanie's disappointment a reconciled memory. But except to eyes of faith, no one in the world would ever know it.

GOD'S COMPANIONSHIP AND GOD'S FRIENDSHIP

We are not alone in the world, and stories like those of Sara and Stephanie are brightly illuminated by the metaphor of Immanuel and the images of God's companionship and friendship.

God is with us, and as surely as God was in Christ, God was with this young woman as she struggled with a missed opportunity.

God's constant presence takes the shape of companionship. The word *companion* itself combines the Latin *panis,* meaning "bread," with the prefix *com,* meaning "with." A companion is a friend who breaks bread with us, one who joins us at mealtime.

John's Revelation puts it this way:

> Behold, I stand at the door and knock; if anyone hears my voice and opens the door, I will come to them and eat with them, and they with me. (Rev. 3:20)

Even though there are now 5 billion of us in the world, God is closely attentive to every one of us. God was a companion to this young woman, and he was a companion to Sara, just like he was a companion to those on the road to Emmaus (Luke 24:13ff.). Companionship is a sterling image for God's love. It is evident in the Last Supper, in every other meal Jesus shared with his disciples, and in every Holy Communion the church has celebrated since.

Stephanie had no idea that her disappointment was of cosmic interest. But that did not stop God from doing what God loves to do best of all: make communion in a broken universe. The fact that her volleyball coach took a lunchtime seat close to her mother, even though other chairs were nearby, signs God's companionable interest.

The Bible has a great deal to say about God, but little outshines these ideas. The Book of Common Prayer adds to these perspectives:

> O heavenly Father, in whom we live and move and have our being: We humbly pray you to guide and govern us by your Holy Spirit, that in all the cares and occupations of our life we may not forget you, but may remember that we are ever walking in your sight. . . . (Book of Common Prayer, p. 100)

Shattered hopes also have a way of cutting all of us off from the sources of support we have learned to depend upon. So upon hearing the news, Stephanie felt painfully alone. But God was present, and the quality of God's companionship is sharply described in the Old Testament book of Ruth.

At first glance the short book of Ruth seems to be little more than a love story about several people: Ruth; her mother-in-law, Naomi; and Naomi's distant relative, Boaz. Because all three are the distant forebears of Jesus, one might think this is the reason for its inclusion in the Bible. But there is more. The book of Ruth is fundamentally a story of God himself.

The word *Ruth*, in Hebrew, means "friend." And the word *Naomi* means "my joy." *Friend* offered to stay with *my joy* when she considered returning to her home, Jerusalem, and these are her words:

> Entreat me not to leave you or to return from following you; for where you go I will go, and where you lodge I will lodge; your people shall be my people, and your God my God; where you die I will die, and there will I be buried. May the Lord do so to me and more also if even death parts me from you. (Ruth 1:16-17, RSV)

God has cast his lot with us, and the book of Ruth simply illustrates this truth with a love story. Here is friendship to be reckoned with, and the words in these two verses echo Jesus' yet to come ministry.

A friend is not abusive, nor is a friend ruthless. A friend is one who acts on affection, one who provides for us when we cannot provide for ourselves. God is this kind of a friend and much, much more.

STORY 3. A CHILD IS KILLED

Fortunate coincidence is fun to work with. But what do we make of the tragedies that also mark human life? Why do bad things happen to us if God is so good? The following story paints a solicitous picture of God's love following the death of a youngster struck and killed by a drunk driver.

By no stretch of the imagination can one say that God wants us to drink and drive. Intoxication is too much of a risk, and the more intoxicated we become, the more likely we are to wreck our lives and those of others. But we are free (are we not?) to drink as much as we want. And even if a still small voice thunders, "That's enough," we are free to listen or not.

When working with stories of tragedy I pay particularly attention to three items:

—our freedom to do things selfishly,
—sin as our God-given capacity to turn away from God's interested-in-us conversation, and
—I am always sensitive to God's powerlessness and the work of the Adversary of Scripture.

Now the story. Richard Morsilli's thirteen-year-old son, Todd, was walking with a friend along the roadside following a tennis game. A weaving car hurled toward them. Todd's friend was able to jump into a nearby snowbank, safely out of the way. But Todd could not jump, and he died on the spot.

Later, Mr. Morsilli was asked to speak to the students of nearby Riverdale Country School. He was asked to talk about drunk driving from the perspective of a victim's parent.

As you can imagine, Mr. Morsilli struggled with what to say. But he must have said it well because of the response. We pick up the story at the end of his talk that day: "I guess that's all I have to say. Thank you for listening." Then Richard Morsilli offers, just to us, some of his private thoughts as the students press forward to greet him.[2]

> Did I say enough? Did I say too much? Why, they're applauding. They're all standing up. That fellow is coming up on the platform. He's holding out his hand. They're lining up. Are they all going to shake my hand?

> * *

> "Thank you. I'm glad I came, too." "No, she didn't go to jail. Her three-year sentence was suspended. Her probation terms included regular psychological counseling, work at a halfway house and no drinking. And her driver's license was suspended for five years."
> "Thank you. Take care of yourselves. All of you, please, please, take care of yourselves."

But Richard Morsilli left out one event, though in the middle of his presentation he briefly considered telling it. I believe this one event signs God's redemptive ministry, making—as best God can— everything all right in an incredibly broken world. You be the judge.

Morsilli continues with his private thoughts.

> What nice kids they are. I think if I'd told them about the fox they'd have understood. They'd have appreciated how astonishing it was, when we'd never seen a fox before, to have one come and stand on the patio two days after Todd's death—just come and stand there staring at the kitchen window before it turned and slowly moved away.
>
> Carole's pregnant sister came to be with her that afternoon. "I've been looking at a book of baby names," she said. "Did you know when you named Todd that his name means fox?"
>
> Was Todd trying to tell us he's all right? I think these kids would understand how much we want to believe that.

How is the pain of a family's loss redeemed? Does it depend only on time and memories grown dim?

What we have is this. A fox in the woods takes one path and not another. An open space shows itself, and maybe because it seems safe (which it was) the fox steps out. Next, another sees and, still later, another offers a word of explanation. And we are left to wonder.

Richard Morsilli is touched by a mystery. His poignant plea signs it. Because of the presence of a fox, senselessness is redeemed a bit. How simple it is.

No one but God redeems like this, not random chance, not good luck, and not good fortune. God offered the Morsilli family the possibility of solace and hope, working with a fox who was just as free as we are to listen to God's counsel, or not.

Look for decision points if you decide to treat this story as drama, and then break it into several scenes. A first scene might take place at the bar, as an unknown driver considers "one more for the road." Perhaps there was a neighbor there who offered to drive her home but was refused. Use your imagination.

Another scene might be the road itself. Why did the boys end up at this place at this time? Was God a passive participant as this driver wheeled her car over the top of the hill? Or are there other alternatives? And what of the Adversary's part in this drama?

Still another scene might involve a fox stepping from the safety of forest cover into a suburban neighborhood's backyard. What of God's participation, or does God just work with human beings? St. Francis would say otherwise.

Stories of tragic events offer the possibility of powerful, theological drama. I hope you are beginning to see some of the opportunities they present.

STORY 4. TOUGH LOVE THAT LOVES US YET

By now you should be able to see how even stories from magazines and newspapers provide vehicles for superb Christian education. Simply look for turning points as the signs of God's ministry they are likely to be and then make interpretation for biblical perspectives. In addition to Mr. Morsilli's story, the one that follows also illustrates this kind of education.

As opposed to an enforced peace, or what we call the peace of Rome (the *Pax Romana*), God wants shalom peace in the world, a wholesome and welcoming peace. And if the *Pax Romana* is imposed by one group of human beings on another, in the face of this injustice God will, with a grieving heart, destroy. This godly action was true for the Hebrews in Egypt, and it is just as true in the same circumstances today.

Like the preceding three stories, what follows is a story about an individual. So it lends itself to an informal play. But this story also describes a worldwide drama, and directly touches the pages of history.

TEACHER WAGING CLASSROOM WAR
AGAINST RACISM

That's what the newspaper headline read. And the article that follows describes a young woman's ministry to a country she loves.[3]

The dateline is Durban, South Africa.

> The memory makes Louise van der Poel wince. "We didn't talk about politics a great deal when I was a teenager," she said. "But I remember vaguely having a discussion in my last year of school, talking about taxes. Someone said blacks don't pay taxes. And I said "—she slips into a squeaky, indignant voice—'Then they get free medical attention!' "
>
> "That was my response. What an awful thing to say. I'm embarrassed to have you write that down."
>
> That conversation took place about nine years ago, when Louise was a politically naive girl of 17, about to take the giant step from the rural village where she grew up to the big university in Durban: nearly 90 miles on a map, light years distant in every other respect.
>
> Now Miss van der Poel, 26, teaches other young girls. And, between pages of Charles Dickens' novels and Sylvia Plath's poems, she tries to prod them to think about South Africa's racial and political troubles in a way she did not. She is an unabashed opponent of apartheid, of military conscription, even of the educational system in which she teaches.
>
> Depending on how you feel about South Africa's unrest, Louise van der Poel has become either part of the solution or part of the problem.

Why did Louise van der Poel change her mind, and why is she now more open to mutual respect? The fact is, God will not have one group of people enslaved to another. The Bible is clear: God works with all the world to overcome self-centered power politics, and Louise van der Poel has been listening to God. She may not know it or even believe it, but eyes of faith know otherwise.

GOD'S SPIRIT ACTS

Clearly evident in this article are signs of a better idea and God's patient conversation mobilizing a society toward renewal. We saw the same thing happen when God mobilized the world to action in World War II.

Generating new ideas in the midst of life is the grace-filled ministry of God's Holy Spirit. It is a ministry from God's right hand, and Hans Küng gives us a bit of insight into how God influenced Louise van der Poel.

> Perceptible and yet not perceptible, invisible and yet powerful, real like the energy-charged air, the wind, the storm, as important for life as the air we breathe: this is how people in ancient times frequently imagined the "Spirit" and God's invisible working.
>
> "Spirit" as understood in the Bible means the force or power proceeding from God, which is opposed to "flesh," to created, perishable reality . . . . (God's Spirit) comes upon (us) powerfully or gently, stirring up individuals or even groups to ecstasy, often effective in extraordinary phenomena, in great men and women, in Moses and the "judges" of Israel, in warriors and singers, kings, prophets and prophetesses.
>
> The spirit is no other than God himself: God close to (humankind) and the world . . . . (She) is then not a third party, not a thing between God and (us), but God's personal closeness . . . ." to us.[4]

[*A Note on the Use of the Feminine Pronoun.* Although Küng writes about the feminine in the Godhead sensitively, he does not use the feminine pronoun in this writing. I interpolated it here, for I am all too aware of the many times the masculine pronoun describes God in most Christian literature. Western Christianity is between the ages in this struggle, and what was once so happily—if naively—embraced is now (happily, for many of us) passing away.

The tradition encouraging a use of the feminine is ancient. Though Father and Son are firmly set in Christian thought, the Holy Spirit of God is referred to in Scripture as both he and she. The feminine Hebrew ruach (the breath or spirit of God) also commends this direction, and Jesus describes himself as a hen wanting to gather her brood, Jerusalem, under her wing (Matt. 23:37-39; Luke 13:34-35).]

God's Holy Spirit stirred Louise to a view of life embracing all of humanity as equal inhabitants of the world. She was set free from old stereotypes, and although Louise is a part of a minority of the white minority, she is not alone.

From the time a white South African first thought, "This isn't right," the numbers of those who object have grown. Now occasional demonstrations outside the South African embassy in Washington, D.C., show these numbers are growing around the world.

"But," you say, "what good are these demonstrations?" Here's the answer:

—They sign God's conversational ministry of care,
—they disclose God's handwriting on the wall, and
—these demonstrations allow us an opportunity to join in His ministry already taking shape in our midst.

God is with us and her presence is personal and interested. She stirs us to new possibilities even in the midst of the old. She rustles our consciousness and sparks shivers of life. We can depend on her; we can prepare for her; we can rejoice in her. But she comes, if ever faithful, nevertheless unexpectedly, and Louise van der Poel is a recipient of her care.

Even though the world seems to be ours and only ours, to do with as we wish, in fact it belongs to God, and God is always about the business of setting captives free. Jesus shows us that. And if God, because of freedom in the universe, is powerless in the moment, he is not impotent. So the prophet watches and with terrible fear hopes anew, knowing the Bible's past is prologue to all the world's future.

The wind of God is blowing in South Africa, and we see it sway the people there as a breeze sways the forest. Perhaps the breeze will have its way. But if its way is not had, the wind will come stronger still, and it will not be quiet. If it takes bloodshed to create communion, bloodshed it will be. The time is not yet, not because God wants it so, but because God honors Creation's freedom. But another theme has already sounded its note in that country, a symphony is building in the background, and this symphony is not one scored by a white minority.

Stories of global events show God's hand at work in the world, and even if they don't lend themselves to the kind of informal drama that makes for good teaching, drama can focus on individuals like Louise van der Poel, while the larger picture can be presented by lecture and then discussed.

PROVIDING CREATIVE CHRISTIAN EDUCATION

Don't miss an opportunity to help adults and teenagers evaluate their ideas about God's presence and ministry in the midst of life.

The following list catalogs the images and metaphors used in this and the last chapter. They can of course be used when discussing any Bible story. But when you use any story of any kind, look first for *turning points*, and then consider the shape of God's action in response to human need and the opportunity presented for ministry.

—God walks with us and talks with us.
—The dialogue between human spirit and God's Holy Spirit.
—The shape of human consciousness and the godly conversation.
—God's grace invites our attention.
—Sin in response to God's ministry.
—Freedom in the universe.
—Discerning Spirit's hope for us: Prayer in action.
—The powers of darkness.
—Human selfishness.
—God's love and God's powerlessness.
—Begin With Coincidence: Luck Or Chance, Or Something More?
—The pillar of fire and the pillar of cloud.
—Providence.
—Altars to an unknown God.
—God's companionship.
—God's friendship.
—God's Spirit Acts.

But like any method of Christian education, this chapter's approach can become "old" with overexposure. So use it judiciously, as one method among the many suggested in this book, and you will provide the kind of variety that makes good Christian education creative and encourages adults and teens to return for more.

Notes

1. John Knox, *The Interpreter's Bible*, vol. 8. (New York, Abingdon Press, 1952), p. 199.

2. Richard Morsilli, "I Still See Him Everywhere," *Reader's Digest* (July 1984): 33-37.

3. Glenn Garvin, "Teacher Waging Classroom War Against Racism," *Washington Times*, October 23, 1985.

4. Hans Küng, *On Being Christian* (Garden City, NY: Doubleday, 1976), pp. 468, 489.

CHAPTER TEN

Building a Mighty Term-Ending Festival

All five terms recommended by *CEME* point toward term-ending show-and-tell festivals. By this point in Part II you should have a good idea about how much material and activity would be available for celebration.

Everyone loves a party, so never miss an opportunity to help your parish celebrate what fun Christian education is; for if you don't, it won't be. Term-ending festivals are especially powerful events in the support of creative Christian education. Here's why.

First, these festivals supply a place to show-and-tell the results of classroom explorations. Children and teachers are given a special opportunity to present their classroom's life and work to the Lord.

Second, they also provide teaching personnel with a Sunday morning break. They put a joyful end to one term and it's theme, while they provide a clear point of departure for the next.

These festivals also provide a *third* benefit to the Sunday morning classroom: they provide a goal toward which to work.

POINT: Goals are made more purposeful when there is an opportunity to display some of the work of the classroom.

MAKING INITIAL PLANS FOR THE SHOW-AND-TELL FESTIVAL

"But," you ask, "when do we make plans for these festivals?" Some churches like to plan the festival before making any classroom plans, and then develop their six-week lesson plans with festival hopes in mind. Other churches choose to develop the six-week term first, knowing full well that the festival itself will offer an opportunity to show-and-tell whatever is explored in the weeks before.

POINT. You can begin with the festival and plan backwards, or you can choose to make plans for the term and simply let the festival give expression to what happens. One way is as good as the other.

BUILDING A CATHEDRAL

Every Christian loves a celebration, and counting each term's length, every festival is under construction for at least six weeks. As the weeks fly by, an atmosphere of parish camaraderie develops. A cathedral is built, not from stone and mortar, but from everyone's anticipation.

The Epiphany term lends itself to explorations of such topics as Jesus' life and ministry, and the life and ministry of your parish and denomination. Light for the world is Epiphany's overarching theme, and with just a little imagination, cathedral worship on "See and Believe" Sunday (taking its name from the Gospel lesson always appointed for that day) can take a bright, "I'll always remember this" shape.

The All Saints festival lends itself to a great procession of old-time and modern day saints. And with careful plans and directions and a printed order of worship, clock time needn't be inordinately extended. Illustration 11 catches just some of the excitement generated at times like these.

The Christmas festival can be built around the pageant with attendant carols, and still later in the year Palm Sunday lends itself to a dramatic congregational reading of the passion Gospel. Some parishes even provide a donkey for the day. Music can be nicely enhanced by a trumpet and maybe even timpani or strings. Use your imagination.

And what can we expect of God's ministry in these moments? An eighty-year-old parishioner puts it this way, with a twinkle in her eye:

> You know, these children aren't learning what I learned in Sunday school. All I remember is that I didn't like it.

In the life of one older Christian, God redeemed a memory and made things new at eighty. God is good.

11. All God's Children: Forming a Procession

(by Gretchen Wolff Pritchard)

THE BOTTOM LINE. Worship is an event through which God announces his presence and sharpens our knowledge of it, and when wedded to the Sunday morning classroom, the two become life-changing agents.

PROVIDE A CAREFULLY CONSTRUCTED BULLETIN

Folks will be present at these festivals who are not a regular part of parish life, so at least a few members of the congregation will be somewhat "new" to one another. They will be looking for careful directions so that they can fit in.

Since it is difficult to juggle several books, especially in unfamiliar patterns of worship, on festival days print out completely the order of worship, including the text of hymns, lessons, and prayers.

Although meaning more work for the office staff, using 8½ x 14 inch sheets of paper, both sides, allows a printed order of eight pages on four sheets.

POINT. A mimeographed order of worship proves especially helpful when many people are involved in complex choreography. Complete with every hymn, prayer, and reading, along with carefully constructed explanations, this order of worship provides for easy dispatch without confusion and hurry.

PLANNING THE LITURGY

Festival, or what I also like to call cathedral worship (as distinguished from every Sunday "house" style worship) can't be overly long. One hour and a few minutes is more than enough time, for when festivals draw out to a greater length, they become more of a task than a celebration.

If festival worship includes the eucharist (which I think it should), the portion of the festival prior to the offertory offers itself for a show-and-tell time.

On festival days, be willing to dispense with the sermon. "Whoa," you say. "Clergy are not going to be willing to give up a sermon are they?" Clergy are more flexible than you may realize, if you are able to make a good case about why these term-ending festivals are important.

Let me discuss festival planning from the top. Always begin with a joyful and upbeat hymn (like "For All the Saints" at the All Saints festival). Form an important procession if possible. Use the procession to demonstrate some of the results of the classroom, and expect the procession to build enthusiasm and joy.

Next move quickly to the Bible lessons appointed for the day. Think about including a brief homily that draws the action of show-and-tell to a focus. Dispense with the creed, the confession, and absolution, and you will have a twenty-minute time period for a show-and-tell presentation. The Prayers of the People can then provide a natural preface to the peace.

When you construct the bulletin, be sure to identify which class is presenting what and, if there is to be a formal presentation, the order for it. See illustration 12 for a work sheet to help you with your planning.

POINT. Make every effort to help everyone, particularly clergy, know what is taking place in the festival and what happens next. An order of worship is designed to bring order to complex things and to make the unfamiliar familiar. If you construct your bulletin with

12. Work Sheet: planning show-and-tell worship

Prepare to abbreviate either Rite I or Rite II of the eucharist in the Book of Common Prayer, or use An Order for Celebrating the Holy Eucharist on page 400. As required by the rubric on page 400, your plans have been carefully made, for most of the congregation has been involved in developing this liturgy for at least six weeks.

Show-and-Tell Introduction

In an opening paragraph explain what will happen and why. Give the rationale for cathedral worship, and be sure to include the names of those who will show-and-tell. Also remember to insert directions at those places where people unfamiliar with this pattern of worship might feel lost.

The Opening Hymn

Always begin with a joyful and upbeat hymn, form an important procession to demonstrate some the gifts from the classroom, and expect the procession to build enthusiasm and joy.

Opening Prayers and Collects

Include as appropriate the announcement of God's presence and prayers, paying attention to the Collect for Purity, the Kyrie and the Collect of the Day. But remember, the more items you include, the more clock time is lengthened.

Reading the Bible

Read the Bible lessons appointed for the day, and conclude with a brief homily that draws the action of show-and-tell to a focus.

The Show-and-Tell Component

In lieu of the creed, confession, and absolution, show-and-tell what the Sunday school has done the previous six weeks. Be sure to identify which class is presenting what and, if there is to be a formal presentation, the order for it.

The show-and-tell component in the service can also come at the time of the offertory. But I prefer to connect it more closely with the lessons, for each of these presentations is an expressions of God's good will and good news today.

The Prayers of the People: Briefly stated, or included at the Offertory.

The Remainder of the Liturgy

Plan the peace and offertory, make eucharist and communion, and close with a prayer of thanksgiving and a rousing final hymn. Finally, make plans for a splendid party in the parish hall for everyone.

this purpose in mind, it will probably contain everything that is said and needs to be said.

Few parishes would be able to tolerate this kind of extravagant worship on a weekly basis. And, in truth, then it might lose its specialness. But because cathedral show-and-tell worship is extravagant, and because it is offered to God only on occasion, it deserves all the careful planning it requires.

EPISCOPALIA

Many denominations do not encourage children to share occasional Sunday morning worship in the way these festivals propose. This is changing, however, as Christian educators point out the opportunities lost when such is not the case.

The flexibility allowing for the development of these festivals is provided, for Episcopalians, in an Order for Celebrating the Holy Eucharist (p. 400 of the Book of Common Prayer). Although this order is not intended for use at the principal Sunday service of the Holy Eucharist, for good reason it can be used. Show-and-tell term-ending festivals provide just this opportunity and the careful preparations required by this order proceed naturally from each term's learning.

Still, Christian education in the Episcopal Church labors with an already in place Prayer Book that does not readily support the construction of show-and-tell worship.

POINT. The Episcopal Book of Common Prayer was not written by Christian educators interested in fitting worship to small children or the classroom. It was written by adults for adults.

I believe this will change when next the Episcopal Church revises its Prayer Book, and in saying this, I'm not making a pitch for baby-talk liturgy or simplistic worship. But next time, I believe that quiet rubrics and directions will be developed to point out opportunities for the occasional inclusion of Sunday morning Sunday school celebrations. As a result, life in the Sunday school will be more effectively honored by the Book of Common Prayer, and the book itself will more accurately reflect this church's love for the education of her young.

But until the future becomes present, the flexibility allowing for the development of these festivals is provided in an Order for Celebrating the Holy Eucharist, page 400 of the Book of Common Prayer. So you need not wait for a revised Prayer Book before you take action to bring your Sunday school before God's Throne of Grace in the nave of your church building.

STANDING ROOM ONLY

Expect your festivals to generate a packed house, and cancel classroom activity on these days. In the place of classroom education, provide a reception in the parish hall for everyone, and you will find that the atmosphere generated by God in worship will continue for another hour or so. Nobody rushes to go home while a good party continues. And because these occasions also enable God's people to begin to know one another more personally, name tags always ought to be used. And they should be given out when hands first reach for the bulletin.

PART III

Making Plans for Successful Christian Education

Troubleshooting Your Size Church: Finding Solutions to Your Problems with Christian Education

Having by now read the first three parts of *CEME*, you're probably at a place of wanting to make specific plans. But some worries may linger. "We just can't seem to get our Sunday school program together" is one comment I often hear. "We're too small to have a Sunday school" comes a word from another. And, "How can we make our Sunday school more of a joyful community, because right now folks are calling it a grind?" says the rector of one large three-hundred member Sunday school.

POINT. Successful Sunday morning Christian education is built around good organization, and there are no "ifs, ands, or buts" about this fact. When organization is carefully developed, and when organization reflects the special needs and opportunities inherent in the size of your congregation, your Sunday school program will grow joy and satisfaction like an English garden grows flowers.

This chapter is designed to help you think through the special opportunities and problems that your size church faces in Sunday morning Christian education, and it takes advantage of a study discussing four congregational models. Illustration 13 shows a problem-solving work sheet to help you diagnose your difficulties and find solutions. So read this chapter with your parish in mind. For every problem there are several solutions, and you will find one that's right for you.[1]

POINT. The size of any church, whether large or small, is good news when we acknowledge the inherent possibilities and opportunities before us. Church size is bad news when we do not.

THREE COMMON PROBLEMS

When developing a Sunday morning program that includes everyone, several common problems often surface.

First, if children are now welcomed into worship, or if Sunday morning worship is now allied with the classroom, matters of discipline and schedule become issues. Questions like, "How can we keep the kids quiet?" and "When should we have Sunday school if not during the time of church?" and observations like, "We can't have noise during the sermon" begin to form. These three concerns are addressed in chapter 6 of *Creative Christian Education,* and practical suggestions are offered as a guide.

Second, including very young children in the eucharist also poses some logistical problems. "How can we include the children in Holy Communion and expect them to behave for an hour and a half?" is the way one person puts it. This question is also addressed in chapter 6 of *Creative Christian Education.*

Parishes struggling with the issue of including young children in the eucharist are doing so because they know that God uses Holy Communion as a means of powerful education. These parishes know it is God's table, not ours, and that God's ministry must be valued more so than our opinion about what is right and what is wrong. These congregations no longer see God as passive or distant at the rail, but are coming to value God as the teacher Jesus reveals God to be, one acting in our behalf long before we know it or know we need it. The issue of young children and the way God uses the eucharist to develop Christian faith is explored in chapter 3 of *CEME.*

Third, many Sunday morning programs of Christian education suffer because the congregation itself has no idea about where the nine-month journey leads and no way to set goals and objectives. Part III in *CEME* is designed to help you set just the kind of goal you need to make your Sunday morning program work well.

MAKING THINGS WORK

In the following pages look for the model closest to the size of your church. Keep in mind your own program and its problems as you read through the following pages, and you will find your difficulties are shared by many. But you will also find more alternatives than you ever guessed possible.

The problem-solving work sheet shown in illustration 13 is designed to help you organize your new ideas, so make notes on it while you read through this chapter.

13. Work Sheet: Solving Problems You Didn't Think You Could

Year_____

This work sheet will help you organize the ideas in chapter 11 that make best sense to you. Use questions 1-4 to make notes as you read through this chapter, and when you have collected your thoughts, organize them with questions 5-7.

1. What size church model most closely fits your church?

2. What are the two or three most important problems you face in your Sunday morning educational program?

3. What ideas strike your interest as you read about your church model in this chapter?

4. Note the ideas that strike your interest as you read about other church models in this chapter.

5. List your new ideas in the order of their importance, most important to least important.

6. What problems can you anticipate when you seek to implement these ideas?

7. Where can you find help in the parish to implement these ideas?

THE FAMILY-SIZE CHURCH

The family-size church is small. Some may even call it tiny. In many cases it has no Sunday morning educational program, and when the possibility of Sunday morning Christian education is considered, members are quick to say, "We need to grow a little larger." But the family-size church probably will not grow until an educational program is in place.

Less than fifty people attend the family size church on a typical Sunday, and if there is a church school, from one to fifteen children are involved in it. Members in this size church may joke that "there are no skeletons hidden in our closet. We know everything there is to know about one another." And they do.

This family-size church depends upon strong lay leadership. Clergy may come and go, but the parish lives on because it is comprised of a people of God who are committed to ministry. The priest in this size parish may divide his or her time between several such congregations.

POINT. Christian education in the family-size church must take into account the following factors.

1. Clergy are often part-time and may be employed in secular work. They may be also responsible for two or more congregations, and because of time and energy, they may not have a high need (or the ability) to influence decisions. The turnover of clergy is often more frequent than that of the laity.

2. Programming is generally centered around an interested lay leader or leaders. If there is no lay leadership interest, there will probably be no program.

POINT FOR EDUCATION. The development of a Sunday morning church school program in the family-size church will depend upon the spark-plug interest, commitment, and enthusiasm of key lay people, perhaps the parents of the children of the parish. Teaching leadership rests in the hands of interested and committed adults who informally plan their interesting programs on the backs of brown bags after church on Sunday or over the telephone during the week.

3. Difficulties facing the small church may include limited resources: people, money, space, and few printed materials or curricula.

POINT FOR EDUCATION. There are numerous already present resources in every congregation, and *CEME* shows many of them.

4. Worship and social times provide the major focus for celebrating parish life, and they are frequently led by ordained leaders.

POINT FOR EDUCATION. The five terms proposed by *CEME* and *Creative Christian Education* build on this strength by ending each term with a show-and-tell festival and parish party.

5. Because of the small size of this parish, intergenerational education is the best way to proceed with Sunday morning Christian education. Please see chapter 2 in *CEME* for directions.

POINT FOR EDUCATION. Intergenerational education is education not by age but by group, and the intergenerational classroom contains "students" from five to one hundred years of age.

With this wealth of persons you are right to do the following:

—Explore with drama a few of the Bible stories appointed in the Sunday morning worship lectionary.

—Choose a parable, work out a skit on it, construct a simple set and/or provide costuming. The play *Godspell* is a perfect illustration of the power and wonder inherent in events like these.

Interage education can involve, not only families with their children, but adults who no longer have children at home.

THE BOTTOM LINE. Of the four churches described in this chapter, I believe the family-size church offers the possibility of the most creative and personally satisfying Sunday morning educational program.

THE PASTORAL-SIZE CHURCH

From fifty to one hundred fifty people attend the pastoral-size church on a typical Sunday morning, and there are from 10 to 40 children in the Sunday school.

In contrast to the family-size church, clergy leadership forms the center of life in this size church. This is why. Because of its size, parishioners may not know everyone else, but they all know their minister, and through their clergy they find their common identity. In large measure it is the pastor who gives focus to the ministry of this size parish.

Lay leadership in the pastoral-size church forms in relation to clergy leadership, and Christian education in the pastoral-size church must take into account the following factors.

1. Clergy involvement and support is essential. If clergy are not interested in Christian education, Christian education will not flourish.

POINT FOR EDUCATION. If clergy leadership does not have the time or interest, both *authority to design the program and support for its implementation* must be enthusiastically given to spark-plug-type people who do want such a program.

2. If there is clergy support, a Christian education committee is probably charged with week-by-week planning and oversight.

POINT FOR EDUCATION. The enthusiasm of adults provides the fuel that causes this educational engine to run, so choosing and supporting the Christian education committee in the pastoral-size congregation is a particularly important task.

It is not likely that this size church will employ an educational specialist, so support for the Sunday morning program will necessarily lie in the hands of this committee.

They will probably work with and directly control a small budget generated by the whole parish. But just as it is done in a few family-size churches, some pastoral-size churches may levy a modest fee for those enrolled in the church school, with scholarship help readily available.

3. There are probably enough children to have a few age-grouped classes, but intergenerational learning is still a best bet on many occasions. There will probably be a volunteer superintendent and a few teachers who have committed themselves to teach for the year, and they are probably all attached to the Christian education committee in some way or another.

4. Sunday school programs in this size parish often struggle to find adequate space, and probably there are some difficulties with teacher recruitment and a low budget. Written curricula materials may not fit the age groupings that are present.

POINT FOR EDUCATION. The five terms proposed by *CEME* and *Creative Christian Education*, a commitment to telling a few Bible stories every year, and the use of parish resources and occasional show-and-tell celebrations, all are made to order for this size parish.

5. If there is adult education, it is often provided by the minister in charge, and its content will generally reflect clergy interest.

6. The youth program, if there is one, is centered around enthusiastic, interested leaders. And teenagers are often active as helpers in the Sunday morning classroom, particularly when drama and crafts are engaged.

POINT FOR EDUCATION. Part IV of *CEME* lists a number of activities designed to keep the interest of teenagers high during the year.

Because they are larger than the family-size church, the pastoral-size parish is more likely to have a variety of people and resources available, while still maintaining the freedom to innovate.

THE BOTTOM LINE. The Sunday morning program in this size church can likely be divided into two or three discrete classes, one for older children, one for younger children, and one for adults. And the five terms proposed by *Creative Christian Education* provide a method that unifies the studies of all three groups.

Occasional events of intergenerational education also can be constructed, like a parish play involving everyone, perhaps during the Epiphany term. Or, from time to time, older children can present some of their work to the younger children, or both groups may combine to present a bit of drama to the adults. And as well, adults can organize a brief play or skit around a Bible story or parable and share it with the children. The good news method of telling Bible stories makes these events Sunday morning theological education at its best.

THE PROGRAM-SIZE CHURCH

The program-size church is a quantum departure from the first two churches described in this chapter. If family- and pastoral-size congregations are built around personal relationships with one another and clergy, the program-size church revolves around a program.

Sunday attendance in the program-size church will vary between 150 and 350 persons, and in the church school there are probably from 25 to 125 children.

The minister in the program-size church primarily functions as an administrator or coordinator of groups and programs. Clergy who serve these churches often pride themselves on being good facilitators of lay leadership, and lay leaders are often elected to positions of responsibility, or they have been appointed as program leaders.

Christian education in the program-size congregation is usually high on every list of priorities for ministry, and it is marked by the following.

1. An organized church school exists under the oversight of a working, decision-making Christian education committee. Often there is a paid director of Christian education. This person generally has a spark-plug-type personality and can be described as a "people lover."

POINT FOR EDUCATION. It's important to be clear about goals and expectations when a Christian education director is employed: the amount of time expected, the rate of pay, and particularly, the method and time of evaluation and recontracting. These tasks are often delegated to the Christian education committee.

2. Classes are often as closely graded as they are in the public school system, and printed curricula materials designed for this size congregation are bought in abundance. But from time to time this complaint is heard: "Where are we going, and what are we doing?"

POINT FOR EDUCATION. Programming coherence and vision are easy casualties in this busy parish, mainly because every classroom is busily engaged in its own activities. A pace for the journey is the proper antidote, and the use of five terms and their show-and-tell festivals often provides all the help that is needed. With just a bit of creativity the show-and-tell festivals can accommodate all printed curricula materials.

3. A large talent pool of people is available to teach in the church school. But because of the size of the parish and other opportunities for service, Sunday morning Christian education may have to compete for their attention.

POINT FOR EDUCATION. The construction of teaching teams provides an excellent method to enlist the interest of teachers in this competitive atmosphere, and the teams themselves provide a time of fellowship and the satisfaction that are so important in this size congregation. For more information on the development of such teams, see chapter 7 in *Creative Christian Education* and chapter 1 in *CEME*.

Teacher recruitment in this size church needs to go on all year long.

4. There is ample space for Christian education or the ability to provide for it.

5. A commitment is made to teacher training, and there exists the financial muscle to send teachers to training events.

6. Youth groups may constitute a separate program from junior and senior high church school classes, if these exist.

7. Adult education leadership may be shared among clergy and laity, and its content is likely to more broadly reflect the interests of the congregation.

The pace of life in the program-size church is fast, and this congregation will often have energy like that of an adolescent. No problem is too big, and strength seems to be adequate for every task.

But because of this energy there is a tendency to fracture, and parishioners sometimes begin to wonder, "Who's in charge?" A program calendar that pictures the whole year (described in chapter 13) goes a long way toward ameliorating this tendency, just as the pace of five seasons with their festivals also helps.

THE CORPORATION-SIZE CHURCH

The corporation-size church is big, and that poses special opportunities and problems for Sunday morning Christian education. Sunday attendance may reach 350 or more people, and the Sunday school may number dramatically more than 100 children.

The paid staff in this size congregation often consists of several professionals, both lay and clergy. There is a complex organization of governing boards, and primary and secondary leaders.

There is also a high degree of diversity among members of the congregation, often a reason members identify with this size congregation. There may be neighborhood congregations that meet as evening supper or prayer groups.

The senior minister often seems remote from most of the congregation but does serve as a stabilizing force in the midst of their diversity. She or he functions as a manager of the staff and pastor to the governing board.

Sunday school in the corporation-size church looks like this:

1. The senior minister is less visible in the Christian education program. He or she may appear only at major functions like the opening and closing of the school year program.

POINT FOR EDUCATION. Term-ending festivals offer an opportunity for clergy to tie in closely with Sunday morning Christian education, and their presence inevitably strengthens the morale of teachers, parents, and children.

2. There is ample budget, space, and equipment available for Sunday morning Christian education. Teachers may have taught for years, and on occasion some are paid.

3. The highly organized church school functions with a multiple, paid staff. There may be separate Sunday schools connected with each church service, with additional programming during the week.

POINT FOR EDUCATION. In addition to a paid staff, there might be a superintendent, a resource coordinator, a festival planner, a recruiting manager, and a training coordinator. These folks are recruited from the congregation, they serve for a two- or three-year term, and they meet regularly with the Christian education director to do long-range planning and goal setting.

4. The classrooms are closely graded, from prekindergarten through the twelfth grade.

POINT FOR EDUCATION. In this size church, the public school model works well to help this complex organization keep order and make maximum use of its many resources.

5. Adult education is usually led by the church staff or outside speakers who are paid to provide programs that reflect the interests and personality of the congregation. There is an opportunity for every member of the parish to attend a class or forum of their choosing on Sundays.

As good as this sounds, several problems commonly characterize Sunday school programs in the corporation-size church. These problems also appear in the program-size church.

1. Long-range vision is frequently an issue, particularly if off-the-shelf curricula materials are used. Too often these materials are simply parceled out to classroom teachers. Seldom are parish goals and objectives developed. And when parishioners don't know where their educational program is headed or see how its components work together (assuming that they do), frustration results (and frustration generates anger).

The nine-month school year in the corporation-size church can be likened to a wave about to break. We can't stop the movement or the force of the wave (nor would we want to), but if we don't stand just behind the crest of the break and point out where the water will go, instead of a program accelerating with expectant joy it is likely that the program will be washed away.

POINT FOR EDUCATION. The development of a program calendar describing the year's journey is essential for the corporation-size church, and seasonal terms offer a unifying guide that works. They provide a map for the nine-month school year, and term-ending festivals help celebrate the work of the children for the sake of their parents and the wider church fellowship. These items are discussed in chapter 13.

2. Sporadic attendance is also a problem, and a lack of attendance becomes particularly acute when one Sunday's work prepares for the next week's study.

POINT FOR EDUCATION. As much as possible help each week's classroom study stand on its own. The focus given by seasonal terms, the goals and objectives on which these terms insist, and the festivals toward which every term looks forward all provide ties that easily bind consecutive Sundays to one another and make it easy to reincorporate the absent student back into class life.

USING THE PROBLEM-SOLVING WORK SHEET

By now you have likely noted several new ideas on the problem-solving work sheet (illustration 13). If you are troubleshooting with some colleagues, all the better, for more heads are generally better than one when working at tasks like these.

Now talk together about these new ideas, make sure you clearly understand how these ideas will help you solve the problems you face (so that you can explain your ideas to others who have not read this chapter), and think about the way in which these solutions can be implemented.

With these new perspectives in hand, your Sunday morning program is now more likely to be the creative event you've long hoped it would be.

Notes

1. This chapter's discussion is shaped and focused by the thoughts of Barbara Taylor and John Vogelsang expressed in *Sizing Up Christian Education in Your Congregation: A Handbook for Educators*. This draft manuscript was published by the Executive Council of the Episcopal Church in 1987, using the research of the Reverend Dr. Arlin Rothauge, *Sizing Up Congregations for New Member Ministry*. Education for Mission and Ministry, Episcopal Church Center, 815 Second Avenue, NY, NY 10017.

CHAPTER TWELVE

Each Year: Set a Goal and a Few Realistic Objectives

Defining a goal and setting a few objectives are without a doubt the most important ingredients in a successful Sunday morning program of Christian education.

POINT. In the same way that clearly written directions aid the assembly of a complex Christmas present, a goal and some objectives provide important help for Christian educators.

No matter what the size of your congregation, this chapter can help you put it all together. It explains the importance of defining a goal and setting a few objectives, tells you how to share these items with the parish, and provides a work sheet to help you begin.

PROGRAMMING: WHETHER YOU CRASH OR WHETHER YOU FLY

Sunday schools fly or crash on the basis of a dream. So first off, dream a bit about what you want in your Christian education program. One question always begins this task: What do *you* want to happen in your Christian education program in the coming year?

Charles Cook is the vicar of a small church, the Church of the Messiah (Episcopal) in Highland Springs, Virginia. Several years ago he and some Sunday school teachers attended a spring workshop I conducted, and as a result they formulated three objectives for their parish program;

1. They decided to focus their energy on telling a few Bible stories well.

2. They implemented the five seasonal terms and concluding show-and-tell festivals proposed in *Creative Christian Education.*

3. They decided to adhere to the notion that less is more. By doing less on Sunday morning and by having more fun with a few things, everyone feels a greater sense of satisfaction.

After working with these objectives for half a year, Charles Cook writes the following.

> One of the greatest benefits (of what we learned in your workshop) is this: our teachers are learning to cover less material more thoroughly. Comments have come to me about the ability to relax and get into the Bible stories selected for use during the term.
>
> We concluded the All Saints term with a wonderful celebration of the eucharist. The Christmas term ended with our Christmas pageant put on by the Sunday school in the context of the eucharist. The Epiphany-Lenten term will be concluded by Sunday school participation in the Palm Sunday Narrated Gospel, which allows maximum participation of readers and congregation.
>
> As in the introduction of anything new there was some fear and trepidation last fall, but that has been replaced by a new awareness of doing things in a more relaxed way.

I remember Charles Cook and his friends at that seminar. They took careful notes, asked questions, and evaluated what I said against what they knew might work at their church.

Objectives go a long way toward insuring success in Sunday morning Christian education, and although this priest makes no mention of having set an overall goal, "to learn about God through Bible stories" is implicit in the objectives they set before themselves.

MAKING DREAMS REAL

Simply put, a goal is an expression of a dream. So come with me and develop a dream about Sunday morning Christian education, and then work with me to forge this dream into a goal and a few realistic objectives to make that goal real.

The progression runs this way. Dreams lead to goals, and to make goals real we set objectives. A work sheet to help you accomplish this task is found in illustration 14, at the end of this chapter.

POINT. Dream, dream, and dream some more: Always begin with dreams. Dreams are the road maps to the future. Then take your dreams and make them into a bright goal and set a few realistic objectives to get you there.

For example, my dream is this. I want a Sunday school in which God is met and known to be met every Sunday we gather together. I want enthusiasm—*en* (in) *theos* (God) to reign—and joy to be the major classroom characteristic.

"But that's painting a rosy picture!" you say. And you say right. It is a rosy picture. But it is also a dream, and with a dream like this I have a good place to begin work.

The dream might be stated this way; "to enjoy the task of meeting God and getting to know God through the use of Bible stories."

POINT. Let's be clear about this, always include learning about God in your goal for Sunday morning Christian education. Don't simply say, "to have a satisfying classroom experience," or "to have fun on Sunday morning." Too many churches create no more of a goal than this for their educational program. As a consequence their programs suffer, for these two goals are really no goals at all.

SETTING A FEW OBJECTIVES

With a goal in mind, setting a few objectives is next. To honor the goal developed in the preceding section, every year I want my parish to spend some of its time together studying the Bible, to meet and be met by the same God who met folks like Daniel, Sara, David, Samuel, the widow, Ruth, Boaz, Matthew, Stephen, Paul, and the list goes on and on. I want to use the old, old stories in the Bible as vehicles designed to tell a story through which the living God meets us yet. I know full well that the more we meet God in scripture, the more likely we will recognize God's presence in the here-and-now of everyday life.

I also want my parish to value the way God is present in the here-and-now of everyday life, the way God helps us take care of his world through the many occupations that we hold, and the way our parish brings light to our community today. This list goes on and on. The truth is, God is not an idea "out there" or "up there," nor is God far distant and removed from us. God is present in the here-and-now of our lives today, in the same way he was present in Bible times.

These objectives can be refined further, even into one-line phrases such as, "to explore one Bible story in each of the five terms," and, "to make three banners to be hung in church depicting three of the stories."

POINT. Objectives give us practical guidelines, they create a sense of clarity and purpose, and at the end of the year they give us the means to measure how well we did.

> At many conferences I'm reminded to ask participants, clergy, and church school teachers if, with secure assurance, they can affirm that their church learned five Bible stories in the previous year. Few respond positively.
>
> Now, you and I know the Bible is read in church, and we know as well that the Bible is occasionally studied in the classroom.
>
> But something is missing if we can't with assurance look back on our recent past and clearly note what we have been studying for the last nine months. Goals and objectives go a long way to help us out of this mess.
>
> So set a few goals and objectives every year. And while you are setting them, remember not to set too many because the few minutes that we have on Sunday morning mean that we always have to value the notion that less is more.

But don't set so many objectives that everyone is exhausted by the time the year ends. When we load too much into the Sunday morning classroom, frustration generates, boredom builds, and joy diminishes.

A GRAND BEGINNING

The notion of defining a goal and setting a few objectives might be a bit new for you, maybe even formidable. But I hope that won't keep you from considering the task.

Good Sunday school programs are strong on defining a goal and setting a few objectives. When teachers, students, and parishioners have a vision about what's going on and where they're headed over the nine-month school year, and when regularly scheduled special events celebrate the nine-month Sunday morning journey, enthusiasm grows by leaps and bounds.

14. Work Sheet: setting one goal and a few objectives

Year_____

Every parish program works better with a goal in mind and a few objectives in hand. To formulate a goal, put on your childhood shoes and move back into your early memories. Those who don't appreciate their past (and learn from it) are doomed to repeat it.

1. Recall your early experience in Sunday school (if you have one to remember). Now pick one representative experience and prepare to share it with the group. If it is a good experience ask yourself this question:
   —"What touched me most deeply?" Remember this: The word *enthusiasm* is rooted in the Greek *en* (in) *theos* (God), so look for enthusiasm in your memory. Do you recall a special teacher or special event? Share your memory, for those were times in which you were touched by God. These memorable experiences are the kinds of events we want to create for our children today.
   —If your early experience was painful (or simply bland), it still offers good help in the activity of setting a current goal. Look closely at what happened, and be prepared to say to your group how things could have been done differently or better.

2. Next, with these individual memories in mind and shared with the group, begin work on a goal for your Sunday morning program of Christian education. But make it simple and begin with, "To . . ." The more complex your overall goal becomes the less helpful it will be. One Christian education committee summed up their year goal this way: "To have fun learning about God by exploring the Bible."

3. With a goal now set, next develop a few parish objectives to implement this goal. The same church just noted decided that over the course of a year they wanted to learn three Bible stories (which they picked), write a new Christmas pageant, learn supporting hymns, and involve the whole parish in some occasional memory work. In addition they decided to devote one term to an exploration of their history and, if possible, illustrate it with old photographs.

4. Now only the following remains:
   —Share your vision and program with the parish at large, and acquaint teachers with the objectives you have set.

By year's end it will be easy to evaluate the effectiveness of your program. Simply ask your parish what you did during the year just over. Everyone will remember.

PART IV

Using
Creative Christian Education

CHAPTER THIRTEEN

Making Plans for the Year, Each Term, and Every Sunday

This is a make plans chapter, for now that you've caught a vision for creative Christian education, you'll want to make plans for whole year, every term, and each Sunday. But don't expect to complete these plans at one sitting. That's asking too much. To make your task easy, however, sample work sheets to guide you with these three tasks are included (see illustrations 15,16, and 18). Also, see illustration 6, a work sheet about planning the whole year, and see illustration 17, a work sheet about the All Saints term.

Finally, the remaining chapters in this section of *CEME*, Part IV, list ideas drawn from the five terms described in *Creative Christian Education*. Use these resources as you plan your year, and you are not likely to run out of topics or activities to enjoy with your class.

PLANNING THE WHOLE YEAR

The sample work sheet on planning the whole year, shown in illustration 15, will help you assign teaching responsibilities and sketch broad-stroke plans for the whole year.

This work sheet is best completed in the late spring or early summer before the new school year begins. Having careful, broad-stroke plans already in place long before the autumn begins makes it easier to enlist the help of teachers, it generates enthusiasm among parents, and it makes using the "term" and "one Sunday" sample work sheets (illustrations 16 and 18) easy to use.

PLANNING EACH TERM

Once you've planned the whole year, you will want to get to work planning the five terms proposed in *CEME*. A completed work sheet for the All Saints term, based on the "Work sheet: planning the whole year" (illustration 6), is shown in illustration 17.

HELPING YOUR PARISH CATCH THE VISION

Now there's only one last step to take; you will want to help your parish catch the vision you see.

To do this, before September begins, publish a *program calendar* showing your parish what you will be doing in this nine-month school year. It should state your goal and the few objectives you have set, and present the broad-stroke picture you have painted of all five terms and the major events you've planned for the year.

POINT. A program calendar schedules events to make the vision of parish Christian education concrete for everyone.

Your program calendar should begin with a list of late summer teacher's meetings, continue with information about the Sunday morning educational program, and it should list every parish event during the year that pertains to education or hospitality (like evening supper groups, weekly prayer groups, etc). Newcomers, particularly, will be interested in how your educational program functions.

Every staff meeting ought to center some of its interest on the program schedule to date, events should be anticipated in the newsletter Sunday morning announcements, and they should be regularly included in the Sunday bulletin.

POINT. Because of this program calendar, every member of your parish will know what the year offers and, at any point in the year, just where the journey will next lead.

Once the program calendar is in place, it connects the hopes and expectations of the parish to specific events; enthusiasm is fueled with even more energy; and this energy, commitment, and focus provide the foundation for dynamite parish Christian education. Fill in the twelve months with such things as

—the dates for preregistration and registration,

—the dates of the terms,

—the date of the festival,

—the dates of other important worship (a blessing of the animals, etc.),

—the dates for teacher training sessions,

—adult education topics,

—"due dates" for hymns, prayers, or Bible verses chosen to be memorized, and

—newsletter deadlines for Christian education news.

Still other events are these: the recognition of acolytes, the ministry of the vestry, meetings of the board of deacons or stewards, Sunday school registration, a year-end Sunday school celebration, recognition of the basketball team, etc.

Better than I, you know who you are, and your calendar will serve you best if it recognizes the wealth of people and events in your parish.

It may not seem so, but small church programs can also make good use of a program calendar. Although you know that your size offers the gift of informal camaraderie, it's still fun to "see in print and picture" the educational journey you've made plans to enjoy.

One parish calls their year long program calendar

* * THE MAP * *

and their map is brightly painted and displayed in a prominent place.

Another church pictures a railroad train on their parish hall wall, and every Sunday it moves further along its nine-month track. Children are always interested in where it's going next, and because they are interested, so are their parents. You can bet this parish is going gangbusters in their Sunday morning program.

A prominently placed Christian education bulletin board can also serve as a program calendar. It can be renewed every other Sunday to remind the parish of the good news taking place in the Sunday morning educational program, and where the program is headed next.

POINT. A program calendar, a map, a train, and a bulletin board are simply small details in any Sunday school program. But attention to details like these generally separates enjoyable Sunday school programs from those just limping along.

Program calendars are particularly necessary in large-size churches. With so much taking place on Sunday morning and with so many people involved, it's easy to lose the wider picture holding everything together.

USING THE WORK SHEETS

Each of the three sample work sheets (illustrations 15, 16, 18) is designed to make your planning as easy as possible. These blank templates should be photocopied so that they can be used by everyone. (Increase sample work sheet 15 154% on 8½ x 14 inch paper, and increase sample work sheet 16 134% on 8½ x 14 inch paper.) By now you should have every reason to expect that you will easily be able to fill these work sheets with excitement-generating plans, using parts II and IV of *CEME*, as well as *Creative Christian Education*.

15. Sample Work Sheet: plan a whole year

—Goal for the year: _____

—Objectives for the year: _____

_____ to _____
   date   date

Season/Dates	Team members who will teach during this term	Your focus	Resources and activities to make the learning fun
ALL SAINTS			
Starting Date _____ Ending Date _____ Number of Sundays _____ Festival Date _____			*Bible Story:* *Song:* *Memory Verse:* *Activities:*
CHRISTMAS			
Starting Date _____ Ending Date _____ Number of Sundays _____ Festival Date _____			*Bible Story:* *Song:* *Memory Verse:* *Activities:*
EPIPHANY			
Starting Date _____ Ending Date _____ Number of Sundays _____ Festival Date _____			*Memory Verse:* *Song:* *Activities:*
LENT			
Starting Date _____ Ending Date _____ Number of Sundays _____ Festival Date _____			*Bible Story:* *Song:* *Memory Verse:* *Activities:*
EASTER/PENTECOST			
Starting Date _____ Ending Date _____ Number of Sundays _____ Festival Date _____			*Bible Story:* *Memory Verse:* *Activities:*

16. Sample Work Sheet: plan a term

Term/Year _____

Number of Sundays in this term _____

Now we are ready to make specific plans.

There are six categories in the following work sheet. Each is designed to help you think about every Sunday in this term.

—The *focus for the day* can be the Bible story you have chosen, a craft activity, a field trip, the discussion of a particular topic, a play, etc.

—*Total time* is an important element in the Sunday morning classroom. Note the time you have, and if you will need to have parents help on some of the craft work at home.

—The *major teachers* should be noted, if you are working as a teaching team.

—The *objective for the day* should be a brief statement about what you want your students to "have" when the day is over. It may be something as simple as "fun," as concrete as a banner, or as important as a new understanding of how close God is in the midst of life. If you have an objective, the chances are good that you and your students will achieve it if you use the methods proposed in this book.

—The category of *Arts/Crafts/Drama/ Discussion* reminds you to involve your students in the subject with "playful" activities.

—*Resource books and page numbers* is a category designed to help you remember where you found that good idea you like so well, so you won't forget.

Focus: What will you do?	Total time available	Major teachers	Objective: what do you want your students to learn?	Arts/Crafts/ Drama/Discussion	Resource books, & page numbers
First Sunday (date) _____					
Second Sunday (date) _____					

Third Sunday (date) ———	Fourth Sunday (date) ———	Fifth Sunday (date) ———	Sixth Sunday (date) ———	(date) ———	(date) ———	(date) ———	(date) ———

17. Work Sheet: the All Saints term

Elementary School Children in a Small Parish or Mission

by

Jim, Joy, and Carolyn

YEAR B

Number of Sundays in the All Saints Term: 8

Saints Who Promote Healing

Focus: What will you do?	Total time available	Major teachers	Objectives: What do you want your students to learn?	Arts/Crafts/ Drama/Discussion	Resource books & page numbers
FIRST SUNDAY: 9-11-88 Teachers will greet family members and children and chat informally. Identify family members.	45 min.	Jim, Joy & Carolyn	They are welcome. Church School will be fun.	Registration, refreshments & exhibits in the Parish Hall.	Mark 9:14-29 CCE, Ch. 5, Bible Study CEME, Ch. 5, pp. 5-7.
SECOND SUNDAY: 9-18-88 Tell the Bible story.	45 min.	Jim, Joy & Carolyn	Understand the there-and-then of story.	Stop-action scenes	CCE, Ch. 9, pp. 108-111 Arch Books
THIRD SUNDAY: 9-25-88 Read the story. Introduce song: "I Sing a Song of the Saints"	45 min.	Jim, Joy & Carolyn	Be aware of saints in the world today.	Repeat stop-action scenes. Discuss here-and-now.	

FOURTH SUNDAY: 10-2-88 Continue singing. Facilitate the drama. Present Bible memory verse.	45 min.	Jim, Joy & Carolyn	Be aware of themselves as saints in the world today.	Recreate the story in the children's language.	
FIFTH SUNDAY: 10-9-88 Introduce visitors: Easily recognized healer/saints, as doctors, rescue squad. Keep singing.	45 min.	Jim, Joy & Carolyn	Day-to-day activities of healer/saints.	Discussion of feelings when sick or hurt.	Notify parents of All Saints Parade and costume-making date.
SIXTH SUNDAY: 10-16-88 Introduce less recognized healers: counselors, sanitation engineers, 911 telephone operators. Keep singing.	45 min.	Jim, Joy & Carolyn	Day-to-day activities of healer/saints.	Discussion of healers they know. Decide on costumes.	Costume-making day for Saturday, 10-22.
SEVENTH SUNDAY: 10-23-88 Facilitate the scenes. Discuss costumes for festival. Keep singing. Review Bible verse.	45 min.	Jim, Joy & Carolyn	To connect saints of there-and-then with saints of here-and-now.	Stop-action scenes depicting today's saints.	
ALL SAINTS FESTIVAL AND PARTY: 10-30-88 Get ready for festival.	45 min.	Jim, Joy & Carolyn	To celebrate	Put on costumes. Practice song. Walk through parade positions.	

18. Work Sheet: planning one Sunday for

_____

Term

Total time with which to work in class _____

Minutes

_____

Date

1. Before you use this work sheet:
   —make photocopies for each Sunday you are planning, and
   —work from the term plans you have already completed.

2. The following categories are designed to help you plan for a thirty-plus minute classroom period of time.

   —*Getting started.* An opening exercise is helpful in convening your class and getting their attention. It can consist of remembering the most important thing that happened to them in the week just over (a show-and-tell), a classroom chapel service, praying a prayer they are learning, reciting a memory verse, plunging immediately into the task of Bible drama, etc. You are in charge, and your students are looking to you for leadership.

   —*Implementing your objective for the day.* You have already determined an objective for the day in your term planning work sheet. In order for your students to carry something home, they must be given something. This is a time to be explicit about what will happen today, how it will happen, and why it is important. You may wish to brainstorm with your class about this "why?" question.

   —*The playful activity.* Art/craft/drama/discussion involve your class in what you introduced above. This is celebrational activity, it moves the life of the classroom into a sense of eucharist, and will return your students to you week after week.

   —*Carry-over.* Your students by now may have an item to take home, or you may wish to bring an item for next week. But because sporadic attendance is often problematic on Sunday morning, don't count on their participation. Still, this can be also a "teaser" time, an opportunity to whet their appetite for next week's exploration.

a) GETTING STARTING (5 MINUTES). YOUR TIME _____

b) IMPLEMENTING YOUR OBJECTIVE FOR THE DAY (5-10 MINUTES). YOUR TIME _____

c) THE PLAYFUL ACTIVITY (20-30 MINUTES). YOUR TIME _____

d) ENDING AND WRAP UP (5-10 MINUTES). YOUR TIME _____

e) CARRY OVER.

CHAPTER FOURTEEN

Planning the All Saints Term: All Saints—All of Us

Using *Creative Christian Education*

September's start-up always generates enthusiasm, and this chapter is designed to help you plan the first six-week term of the year, "All Saints—All of Us." The ideas in the following pages are all drawn from a similar, but more expansive, chapter in *Creative Christian Education*.

WHAT MAKES ALL SAINTS FUN?

All Saints is perhaps the most colorful of all five terms. It may be because of fire engines and rescue squad trucks or because of real life saints telling their stories. But no matter how the color is generated, everything is brightened by a grand procession of saints in the early November festival.

Also, remember to publicize items about your Christian education program in your local paper. It may be a human interest story to the press, but it is grand advertising for God's love.

TOPICS AND TASKS FOR ALL AGES

1. Bible stories appointed by the lectionary to be read in Sunday's worship are always appropriate. Both the popularly named

"Colorado Curriculum" (*Living the Good News*) and the *Prayer Book Guide to Christian Education* offer numerous ideas and suggestions about the use of every Bible reading designated for worship on Sunday morning. Both these resources are good aids, and they can be purchased from sources quoted in appendix A, "A Bookstore for You."

2. Study saints today by scheduling the police canine corps, the fire department, or rescue squad members for Sunday visits. Teaching is brightened and made concrete by these visits.

3. The saints of God are remembered on special days called feast days all during the year. Most fall on a weekday, which may be why you never hear much of them. All the major saints', feast days are listed in the Book of Common Prayer (p. 921ff.), and several appear during the All Saints term.

a) St. Matthew (September 21)

b) St. Michael and All Angels (September 29)

> "Where does the devil-talk in the Bible come from?" some might ask. And others may wonder, "Why do bad things happen if God is so loving?" This grand story seeks to provide an explanation. Question: Could you plan a play to dramatize this cosmic struggle?

c) St. Luke (October 18)

> Church legend has it that St. Luke was a medical doctor, and his feast day provides the happy possibility of an exploration of occupational choices for teenagers and parish recognition of all those who serve in the health care professions.

d) St. James of Jerusalem (October 23)

e) St. Simon and St. Jude (October 28)

f) All Saints Day (November 1)

> All Saints' Day provides every kind of encouragement to spend time looking at Christian models who give us guidance today. Saints from the past also encourage us to value the way in which we help God take care of his world today and the way our children will help him in the future.

In addition to these six feast days, there are still more saints' days listed in the remainder of the liturgical year. If your church is named for a saint, the All Saints term provides an opportune time to explore the life and ministry of your "patron."

—St. Andrew

—St. Thomas

—St. Stephen, Deacon and Martyr (see also the Lenten Term)

—St. John

—The Holy Innocents (see also the Epiphany term)
—The Confession of St. Peter
—The Conversion of St. Paul (see also the Epiphany and Easter/ Pentecost terms)
—St. Matthias
—St. Joseph (see also the Epiphany term)
—St. Mark
—St. Philip and St. James
—St. Barnabas
—The Nativity (birth) of St. John the Baptist (see also the Christmas term)
—St. Mary the Virgin (see also the Christmas term)
—St. Bartholomew

4. Much of the Bible read on Sunday morning was written by St. Paul. Many of the studies in the Easter/Pentecost term center on Paul, his conversion, and his ministry of building up the early church. You may wish to include any one of these following themes:

a) St. Paul: Everyone of Us
b) Stories of the Resurrection
c) Stories of Jesus Bringing Life
d) Parables Jesus Used to Explain Life
e) Paul Builds the Church

5. Adopt a shut-in. Along with saints past and present, I hope you'll build ways to include in your plans those older parishioners whom most of us call "shut-in." Though they may not be physically present, your class can remember them at special times of the year by sharing some of the things you're exploring or making in the classroom, such as your pictures or banners.

Should you take this on, part of your task in each term will be that of preparing for your visit. This activity is particularly suitable for classes of small children, but teenagers and adults also find this a benefit.

6. Produce a chancel drama. The Good News Method of telling Bible stories can always generate a play, and Sunday's mainline worship offers an opportunity to present it. I've seen Queen Esther save her people and, on another Sunday, the walls of Jericho came tumbling down. Needless to say attendance dramatically increases for these events.

7. Create a bright banner. The planning and construction of a banner for the term-ending festival is a nice task around which to plan classroom activity.

CAUTION. Please let these creations be as much the children's work as possible. There's a fine line between encouraging them to do their best, helping them develop their talents fully, and taking over the banner yourself. Sometimes the latter may be appropriate, but only in the closing seconds of the eleventh hour.

8. Decide if you would like to have your class decorate the Christian education bulletin board for this term or for the next. What will it show?

9. See the long list of Sunday-by-Sunday possibilities at the end of the chapter describing the All Saints term in *Creative Christian Education.*

CLASSROOM POSSIBILITIES FOR PRESCHOOL THROUGH GRADE SEVEN

Models are important, and this term provides a splendid opportunity to do the following:

1. Study people the church has, through the centuries, designated as good examples for us to emulate.

A class-made banner is a way to illustrate what you learn. A first grade class may wish to make individual banners the size of a sheet of writing paper, because that size is much easier for small people to handle.

2. Help your children begin to learn about the ministry of every member of their parish and the way in which your congregation helps God take care of his world today. An electrician can hook up a simple circuit and describe how she helps God take care of the world, for God's world would be in the dark without electricians. Or an artist can sketch some classroom impressions and talk about the ministry of creating beauty in God's world. Use your imagination.

3. Look at the lives of the most important saints in the lives of your children, their parents. Have them bring pictures of their parents to class for a show-and-tell, pictures back to childhood. Help them also understand how their parents help God take care of the world, at home and in their daily work.

4. Prepare to host the parish All Saints Sunday party, or if this party is already spoken for, host with your children a party in your room for their parents and spend time showing and telling what you did during the term.

5. Prepare the Christian education bulletin board for the All Saints or Christmas term.

Presenting a bulletin board display will fill your classroom with activity, your students will "learn" while they "do," and the enthusiasm beginning to generate in the wider parish will expand.

6. Ask your organist, choir, or members of the choir to help your class learn the "Saints of God" hymn or some other.

7. Ask your clergy to talk to your class about saints.

8. Take your class to church so they can see how the Great Procession on All Saints' Sunday will work.

CLASSROOM POSSIBILITIES FOR TEENAGERS

Right off the bat, review chapters 3 and 4 and the suggestions they make about working with teenagers. Also check out the group activities listed in chapter 7. Do any of those interest you or your teenage charges, or do some of the suggestions listed in chapters 6, 8, and 9 stir your interest? Maybe your class would be interested in putting together several Bible story plays during the year, for presentation to younger children.

What's more, widely used and excellent resources are published by the Zondervan Publishing House, Grand Rapids, Michigan. Their "Youth Specialties" series lists titles like *Far Out Ideas, Holiday Ideas, Way Out Ideas, Ideas For Social Action, Tension Getters,* and so forth. If you need practical suggestions for either your Sunday morning class or the evening youth group, you will probably find them here.

But also attend to the following items:

1. Many teenagers are apprehensive when a new year begins. Social roles are up for grabs, and newness may even generate fears of acceptability to others. At the start of every new year, pay careful attention to community building. Ask them about their hopes for the course, and, if possible, set a few goals for the year.

2. In addition to community building, make plans in September for occasional parties and informal gatherings, perhaps beginning at the teacher's house. But include them in the planning, and as a result the party will become their own.

3. A weekend retreat or a camp-out in the fall, winter, or spring are both good ideas. Neither idea may garner their interest, but if one does, the teenagers and you will have a grand time.

4. Suggest the idea of taking on a few service projects during the year, such as hosting a term-ending party or making plays of a couple of Bible stories to be presented to younger children (help them become

Cecil B. DeMille, and watch out!) or taking on a parish responsibility that needs attention.

5. If possible, try to help connections develop between what you are doing on Sunday morning and what they are doing at the Sunday evening meeting of the youth group. Teenagers, like the rest of us, like being treated as whole people.

6. Part of the "work" of being a teenager is that of beginning to think seriously about future occupations. High school graduation is getting closer.

The All Saints term provides a timely opportunity to help these folks look at the skills they bring to life and Christian ministry and reflect together with adults in the parish who have already made their occupational decisions.

7. A study of saints who lived in the past is also appropriate. As a result of studying Ruth one year, a teenage class put together a magnificent collage on love, using current magazine illustrations. At other times, three-dimensional presentations have been constructed.

8. If asked, your teenage class or youth group would probably be delighted to put on a Bible story play for the younger children, adult class, or the whole church. Expect preparations to be expansive and complex, and expect to have a lot of fun.

CLASSROOM POSSIBILITIES FOR ADULTS

This is the first term of the year, so make every effort to help adults get to know one another. More than a few visitors, alert and newly excited by thoughts of church membership, fall by the wayside when they don't find a welcome sufficient to let them know they've found a home.

Parents and other Christians are keenly interested in what makes Christian education work and how they can help. Many parents, trying to be helpful and scared that by keeping silent their hopes for the children will go unnoticed, request—and on occasion even demand—that Bible passages be memorized as well as the Ten Commandments, the catechism, the Apostles' Creed, and on and on. Recognize their interest, and help them understand how only a few Bible stories studied during the year will do more for their child's spiritual health than any other study. I must also note that never have I stood by the bedside of a dying Christian and had them ask me to recite the Ten Commandments or the Apostles' Creed or the catechism, although they do often ask me to say with them the

Twenty-third psalm or the Lord's Prayer. To help adults understand the shape of faith development and spiritual growth, make use of the study of God's action in chapter 3.

Moreover, explain the year's program that you are about to embark upon. Note the goal and the objectives already set, why they were set, and ask for their consultation. Explain how the use of terms makes the nine-month school year manageable, distinguish the difference between what goes on in the public school and what goes on in the Sunday school (paying particular attention to time constraints and the use of stories of God's action). And pay attention to the special way term-ending festivals give an opportunity for both show-and-tell and blessing.

In addition to the ideas noted in the section of this chapter called "Topics and Tasks for All Ages," and resources listed in appendix A, "A Bookstore for You," adult classes can also do the following:

1. Explore God's ministry in stories from the daily newspaper or their lives.

2. Enter into an exploration and discussion about the way in which God called them to their present occupations and the way in which their daily work helps God take care of his world.

3. Explore their denomination's heritage and the way in which their church is similar to and different from others. This subject always gets a good press from adults.

THE ALL SAINTS FESTIVAL

The term ends with a bang, and the joy of the day emerges from the life, vitality, enthusiasm, and spirited exploration developed as saints are studied by everyone for six weeks.

This term-ending festival offers an opportunity for classes to show-and-tell what they've been studying for the previous six weeks. And the more they show-and-tell, the greater will be the joy and enthusiasm generated in this style of worship.

Now make your plans using the work sheets in illustrations 16-18.

CHAPTER FIFTEEN

Planning the Christmas Term: Out of the Darkness—Light

Using *Creative Christian Education*

This chapter is designed to help you plan the Christmas term. But just as with the All Saints term, don't begin to make every Sunday lesson plans at this point. Simply generate ideas, and later we'll begin to make explicit Sunday plans. The ideas in the following pages are all drawn from a corresponding, but more expansive, chapter in *Creative Christian Education*.

WHAT MAKES THE CHRISTMAS TERM FUN?

The Christmas term best begins on the Sunday after the All Saints celebration. The Christmas holidays are beginning to show on the distant horizon.

But why think of plans for Christmas at this early date? Centuries ago the four weeks of Advent served well to prepare us to celebrate the birth of Christ, but this four-week season is just too short today. With moms and dads both often involved in work-for-pay, with school exams and vacations, gift buying and other family plans, the grand possibilities for unhurried study in the four weeks before Christmas are often lost.

This is what I propose. Begin to anticipate Advent in the three remaining Sundays in November. Some classes may wish to make

Advent wreaths for Advent I. Others may wish to explore the interplay between light and darkness commended by the lectionary during this period, and still other classes may wish to relate the themes of Thanksgiving Day to the Christmas season.

By treating these few Sundays in November as a part of our preparations, Advent and Christmas are more able to offer us their many gifts.

WORSHIP PROVIDES A PLACE FOR CELEBRATION

Parish festivals generate enthusiasm, and this term provides four possibilities not to be overlooked. The first two illustrate the themes of darkness and light that mark the close of the Pentecost season. The third offers an opportunity to present a Christmas pageant. And a fourth suggests the possibility of informal family worship on Christmas Day.

1. The *Sunday of Christ the King* falls on the Sunday immediately before Advent I. Because this is the last Sunday of the Christian year, it marks a grand time to recognize and celebrate the kingship of Christ in the universe.

2. *Thanksgiving Day* also follows at November's end. And on the Sunday after Thanksgiving members of the parish might, along with the church school community, present canned and/or dry goods for distribution through your community's emergency food pantry.

This is also an occasion to note the presence of college students now home for the holidays and the presence of extended families perhaps gathered for annual homecomings.

3. The *Chrismon Festival* is best held on the Sunday before Christmas Day (the last Sunday of the Advent season), and the lesson of focus is always the birth of Jesus. A pageant is the best of all ways to tell it, and children from every grade in the church school, *and adults*, are encouraged to take part.

The pageant itself can be written afresh every year, which makes for good education. Everyone is familiar with Luke 1:26-38 (the story of the Annunciation of Mary), but the story of the Visitation of Mary (Luke 1:39-49) is rarely included, nor is the story of the birth of John the Baptist (Luke 1:13-17, 36-37, 57-60, 80). But don't have the three kings visit. Save this until the Sunday after the Epiphany.

POINT. Festivals provide a place to show-and-tell what you've been exploring in the classroom, and showing and telling provides a grand opportunity for the parish to say to your children, "Well done." As a result, love and affection will reign, and Sunday school will always be fun.

On the day of the Chrismon festival, classroom activity is preempted by a birthday party for Jesus.

4. *Children's worship on Christmas Day* is also a lovely possibility, and a small but increasing number of parishes are celebrating gifts given to the very young by allowing time for showing and telling on Christmas morning or at late afternoon worship. One church calls it the "March of the Toys." But no matter what it's called, enthusiasm abounds and gratitude expands.

But because some of these toys will be too quickly discarded, they might next grace the manger at Epiphany.

5. Look forward to the Epiphany pageant, and don't include the Magi in your Christmas pageant. *Epiphany* is the perfect time for importantly dressed wise folk to make their visit to Jesus. Following in their steps, the children of the parish (as well as parents) can present a leftover Christmas present for use in the pediatrics unit of a local hospital.

As the parish anticipates Christmas, remind your children and adults to set aside a gift or two for an Epiphany presentation at the manger.

TOPICS AND TASKS FOR ALL AGES

If enthusiasm for studies during the All Saints term is still high, capitalize on it. You might be even more specific about how your saints (past or present day) are light for an often dark world. But there are still more possibilities.

1. Bible stories appointed by the lectionary to be read in Sunday's worship are always appropriate. So choose one and deal with it for several weeks.

2. A study of the interplay between light and darkness is particularly appropriate in the weeks before Christmas, and *Creative Christian Education* provides a number of suggestions in chapter 10.

   a) Every worship lectionary uses readings from the Old Testament prophets in the weeks before Christmas, and they in turn often describe God's presence in terms of light. A study of these writings is particularly appropriate in the Christmas term, and

The Prayer Book Guide to Christian Education and Colorado's *Living the Good News* curriculum provide substantial assistance (see appendix A).

b) This term provides an excellent time for the study of hunger in the world and our responsibility in response.

3. The study of the birth of God's light for the world is another always important theme.

a) Prepare an Advent bulletin board about Jesus' birth.

b) Help your class write a Christmas pageant by using the several sections of the Gospels not used.

c) Make an Advent Wreath. It's etiology is explained in chapter 10 of *Creative Christian Education*, and making the wreath can be an inspirational and fun-filled intergenerational parish event. The life of the parish family will be strengthened. Just reserve the parish hall for one Sunday morning, provide directions and supplies, and watch creativity and joy take shape.

d) Encourage family participation in the greening of the church. If you leave this task to the altar guild you are missing an important time to nurture the parish as a family of God.

e) Make Chrismons (symbols for Christ) for three reasons. First, signs and symbols have a way of communicating life's deepest expressions. Second, as we share ourselves with one another in a common task around a common conversation, fellowship grows. And third, Chrismons add a special note of beauty and participation on the day the Christmas pageant is presented.

Set aside one Sunday and construct an intergenerational event to make these Chrismons. Spread tables in the parish hall with all the necessities, encourage creativity, and set one table with coffee, apple cider, cookies, and pastry. It will be a glorious day to remember.

f) Provide a birthday party for Jesus in the parish hall after the Christmas pageant is presented, and invite everyone.

g) Remind children of the "extra" gift to be presented at Epiphany on the first Sunday of the new year, and prepare now to be a part of the team that presents the gifts to the hospital.

h) Continue to include in your plans the shut-in your class has adopted.

i) More suggestions for this term can be found on page 124 of *Creative Christian Education*.

CLASSROOM POSSIBILITIES FOR PRESCHOOL THROUGH
GRADE SEVEN

1. Preparing for Thanksgiving
a) For small children, a hungry tummy sometimes feels a lot like being lost in the dark.
   To have your children feel hunger and talk about it, invite them to come next week without breakfast or sit in class and look at a nice donut for a time. How is food like "light" to hungry persons? Then give them something to eat.
b) Begin to mention the canned goods for the emergency food pantry to be presented on Thanksgiving Day or the first Sunday after Thanksgiving Day.
   Both parents and children should participate in this offering of gifts, and there should be some "extras" at the door so that those who forget can participate.
2. Exploring the interplay between light and darkness.
a) Many young children are afraid of the dark. It represents the unknown, and many of today's horror videos exacerbate these natural fears. God's presence in the darkness is Christian teaching at its best and explains quite clearly why the birth of Jesus means so much to us. In and through Jesus, God offers enlightenment and light to the world.
b) Artists can develop sketches on light and darkness using paint, colored glass, candles, and paper cut outs.
c) Younger children may water paint a small area of paper with yellow and then cover the whole sheet with black crayon. After trading, all try to uncover the "light" by scratching off the "dark," discussing both their activity and their feelings as they begin to see the light.
d) A puppeteer (or a group of teens) can work out a play or plays on light and darkness.
e) Some classes might darken a room, next light a central candle, and then pass its light to candles held by everyone else. This expansion of light is often picked up in an Epiphany Feast of Lights, celebrating the twelfth day of Christmas.
f) Candles and their light have always provided educational emphasis in Christian worship. For a brief discussion, see chapter 11 in *Creative Christian Education.*
g) Blindfolding older students and then talking about the experience as they attempt to perform simple tasks and movements

around a room, "in the dark" as it were, is good education. Question. How does the light of Christ help us move about the world more creatively and easily?

h) Prepare a Christian education bulletin board on light and darkness.

3. Preparing for Christmas.

a) Begin immediately after the All Saints festival to explore the Christmas story, particularly if you are going to make use of any of the many tasks suggested in this term. The Arch Books are big helps with Bible stories, and don't forget to look at the note to parents on the last page of each book. These notes give good ideas about possible lesson plans. See appendix A for more information.

b) Use the choir and organist to learn Christmas hymns and carols.

c) As you study the story of Jesus' birth, make a papier-mâché créche.

d) Jesus had an extended family and so do we. During Advent's Sundays, some classes may wish to explore their own wider families, taking a cue from the Scripture readings designated for Christmas.

Photographs of siblings, grandparents, parents, and friends can be gathered and displayed, perhaps in a collage. This might be the first time a family's heritage has been explored by the children.

e) Small children can also help the wider parish family by participating in the Christmas pageant, and pageant participants ought not be limited to children alone.

If in your Sunday school you have graded classes for children, each class can be asked to provide participants for the pageant. One class could take responsibility for being the angels, another class might provide cut outs of barnyard animals (a few goats, some cattle, a couple of sheep, maybe a dog and cat, as well as one or two camels).

f) Don't forget to make Chrismons for parents, too. Your children can give them as gifts.

CLASSROOM POSSIBILITIES FOR TEENAGERS

1. Adolescents are particularly attuned to injustice in the world and the way in which light and darkness interplay with one another.

Social issues are important, and rightly so. Their high school experience and stories from the weekly newspaper offer important opportunities for them to explore these cogent issues. They will enjoy applying the principles of the Good News Method of telling Bible stories to their life events and stories from everyday life, illustrated in this book's chapters 6, 8 and 9.

2. Older classes might be interested in developing a play for dramatic presentation to the younger children, and some teenagers are skillful with puppets. A puppet show about light and darkness can be a real eye-opener.

3. Perhaps an older class can assist a younger class with a task, providing the "light" of help to both children and teachers. Teachers of small children can certainly use help with making Chrismons.

CLASSROOM POSSIBILITIES FOR ADULTS

1. If there's interest, you can continue the explorations begun in the All Saints term.

2. A study of any one or several of the readings listed in the lectionary is always appropriate, *The Prayer Book Guide to Christian Education* provides summaries of them, and the Good News Method of telling Bible stories along with gospel drama offers the ways and means to make Bible stories interesting.

3. Adults can also participate in the Christmas pageant and model the interest and commitment so important for our children to see. If this is chosen, the adult class will need to spend time preparing for this.

4. Holiday seasons are also a time of stress for many, and for more than a few, this time of the year and the days following Christmas are a time of painful depression. You may wish to develop a program about this, or you may wish to bring in an outside speaker to expand on this important theme.

CHAPTER SIXTEEN

Planning the Epiphany Term: Light for the World

Using *Creative Christian Education*

Some folks say that Christmas is a hard act to follow, and for that reason Sunday morning Christian education often labors when the new year begins. The following paragraphs show why this need not be the case.

WHAT MAKES THE EPIPHANY TERM FUN?

Light for the world is a snapshot description of the Epiphany term, and explorations focus on the world's appreciative response to God's light of Jesus and the gospel, Lent excepted.

This reply can lead to studies of Jesus' life, God's light for the world, communion and community. Your classroom plans are best measured against this study theme.

FESTIVAL WORSHIP

It's possible to begin the Epiphany term with two pageants, and that means enthusiasm is generated right off the bat. There need be no post-Christmas letdown.

1. Because the *visit of the Magi* was anticipated before Christmas, everyone is involved in the Epiphany term before it officially begins. You need expect no post-Christmas letdown, especially if the kings appear in a pageant on the first or second Sunday of the new calendar year.

2. An evening *Feast of Lights* can also be scheduled on the night of the Epiphany or at a more convenient time. It is dramatic worship at its best, and most church musicians can provide ample help if your church decides to make plans for it.

3. The term-ending *See and Believe* festival takes its cue from the Gospel appointed by the common eucharistic lectionary. This is why: because Peter, James, and John were with Jesus when they saw him standing with Moses (the Law) and Elijah (the Prophets), and seeing, they believed afresh that he was the summation and answer to the Hebrew wait for a messiah. In the same way today, when the world hears and sees the good works of Jesus and his Church, the world begins to see and believe.

Your class will probably want to present something in this festival that shows what they "saw" in this term's study and now believe.

Also remember to publicize items about your Christian education program in the local paper. It may be a human interest story to the press, but it is grand advertising for God's love.

TOPICS AND TASKS FOR ALL AGES

This term can encompass numerous Bible stories. But there are other issues also worthy of exploration. Since *Creative Christian Education* suggests many, let your interests and the needs of your students be your guide.

1. Several feast days appear in this term, among them
   —the confession of St. Peter (January 18),
   —the conversion of St. Paul (January 25),
   —the presentation of Jesus at the temple (February 2), and
   —the choice of St. Matthias to replace Judas Iscariot (February 24).

   These festivals are listed in the Book of Common Prayer on page 922, and they can be treated as follows:
   a) If you choose to study one of these three saints during the term, let the theme of light for the world be your guide. Simply tell their story, and let your class explore with questions like these:

—What did these three see in Jesus that was light for the world?

—How and where did they share their knowledge and love for the Lord Jesus?

—What in their lives is light for you and your students now, or in other words, what "turns you and your students on" about their life and ministry?

b) If you choose to study the story of Jesus presentation at the temple, think about constructing a play and learn to sing the Song of Simeon, often called the *Nunc Dimittis*. It's found in the Book of Common Prayer on page 93.

2. A range of additional topics expands Epiphany's theme of light for the world.

a) *Telling the good news stories of Jesus.* Because Jesus cared and because his care was always effective, word of his good works got out to the countryside.

Children and adults can benefit from an exploration of a few of these stories about Jesus, and the good news method of telling Bible stories, when used with teens and adults, becomes substantial theological education. You will also find good help with this topic in Chapter 13 of *Creative Christian Education.*

b) *God's ministry in the birth and growth of Christian faith.* The matter of faith and belief is always an important issue for Christians, but too often God's ministry of birthing and nurturing faith is ignored.

This is a particularly good exploration for adults who are parents, and it can do much to enlighten parental concerns about being responsible Christians. See chapter 4 *Creative Christian Education* and chapter 3 in *CEME* for help.

c) *Children, God's presence and the Holy Communion.* "Why admit children to Holy Communion? They don't understand." This question is closely related to the birth and growth of Christian faith, and answering questions like this finds a good response in adult education. Chapters 4 and 6 of *Creative Christian Education* provide illuminating perspectives.

d) *Exploring baptism and confirmation.* A study of these topics is exactly right for this term. Because God was in Christ in the world, some in the world asked to join his ministry. Many still do.

Epiphany provides an excellent opportunity to review the meaning of baptism or to conduct confirmation and membership classes for those who now want to join the church.

e) *What makes our denomination unique?* I often hear this question asked in all churches: "What makes us different?" There are many helpful books written for every denomination that provide answers, and some are noted in appendix A. I hope you will use them.

f) *The contemporary ministry of our parish church.* Many churches pay scant attention to the helpful ways their membership ministers in the community. But when the work-for-pay jobs of members are considered, it's apparent that the ministry of every local church is incredibly rich. The light of your church deserves to be occasionally celebrated with study, and this term provides a perfect opportunity.

g) *Our parish history.* Every parish began for a set of reasons, and people new to the life of your church will have little knowledge of it unless you tell them. Question: How has your parish been "a light" for your community through the years?

h) *St. Paul's life and ministry.* This is always a worthy study, and this term provides an excellent opportunity for this exploration. *Creative Christian Education* poses an unusual approach in chapter 13.

3. Other topics and tasks combine to commend themselves.

a) What about memory work in this term? Would you like to have your class or the congregation learn a hymn or a Bible verse?

b) Candles and light have always been used by the church to teach about God's love and ministry in the world, and *Creative Christian Education* discusses their use on page 130.

c) The use of seasonal colors is also a teaching device, explained on page 20 of *Creative Christian Education.*

d) More suggestions for this term can be found on page 140 of *Creative Christian Education.*

CLASSROOM POSSIBILITIES FOR PRESCHOOL THROUGH GRADE SEVEN

Exploring a Bible story or a series of stories that tells a larger story (like the birth of Jesus or his growing up) is always appropriate. And once you decide on the Bible story you want to use, you will find the Arch Book series (see appendix A) full of help.

But in addition, consider the following:

1. Volunteer your class to distribute the Epiphany toys given for sick children. But before the presents given at the Epiphany are removed from the church, look with your class at their number and variety, and explore with them how God will use these presents to strengthen the lives of children in the pediatric unit.

2. Continue to include the shut-in your class has adopted.

3. Jesus growing up: a Jewish childhood. Every child has a family, and so did Jesus. By exploring his early childhood your children will deepen their love for him, for he is just like they are. A study of his early childhood will enlighten their lives.

4. Study baptism. Did you know the word *baptize* means "to wash clean"? How is it that we are dirty? Do your children remember their baptism? Are there photographs? Are there any children in your class who might like to be baptized?

5. Study communion. Take your children to church, and let them handle the chalice. Let them practice drinking from it. Use the altar guild to assist your activity. They can show you how the altar and table are set up for the eucharist.

6. Study your church's current and historic ministry. Tour your church building, and invite a member of your vestry or board to talk about the parish.

7. Make a banner to illustrate what you are studying. Know, too, that as your children play while making a banner, they are learning also that God loves them.

8. Create a play for the classroom to share with other classrooms or the adult community, perhaps as chancel drama.

9. Prepare the bulletin board for Epiphany, or look forward to Lent.

10. What will your class present at the "See and Believe" festival?

11. Who will host the term-ending party in the parish hall?

CLASSROOM POSSIBILITIES FOR TEENAGERS

Because a new year is beginning, you may wish to review some of the suggestions made about working with teenagers in the chapter describing the All Saints term, or critique your teaching by using chapter 4 in *CEME*.

During the bleak midwinter, your class might be very interested in exploring stories from the Gospels or from the Old Testament. Gospel drama offers an attractive way for teens to study the Bible, and because the Adversary of Scripture is included and human freedom acknowledged, this method always engenders a lot of lively debate.

But more, when this same method is applied to stories from the daily newspaper or from their everyday life, theological education becomes incredibly powerful.

1. Teenagers may wish to construct and offer a Bible play to the younger children in the parish and learn more about God's love and ministry than they ever would by simply hearing about it in a lecture.

2. Teens may also be delighted to take responsibility for the Christian education bulletin board display during this or the next term.

3. History and current events are always of interest to teenagers, if they are not offered in a lecture format. Help them make a slide presentation or video of their parish's history or current ministry in the community.

CLASSROOM POSSIBILITIES FOR ADULTS

A number of possibilities for study are listed in the "Topics and Tasks" section in this chapter. But particular consideration should be paid to explorations of your denomination's history and the history and current ministry of your congregation.

1. If there is interest, you can continue the explorations begun in previous terms, or maybe some ideas were offered then that you can implement now.

2. The Good News Method of telling Bible stories, gospel drama, and the "Walk-through-Life with God" drama (chapter 9) offer an attractive method of theological education. And when the principles of this method of study are used with stories from everyday life, adult interest will be high.

CHAPTER SEVENTEEN

Planning the Lenten Term: This Is My Son, My Beloved

Using *Creative Christian Education*

While Epiphany's explorations celebrate the world's joyful response to the light of Christ, studies in Lent narrow to the darker side of human nature, and the world's more hostile response to the gospel. But the Easter festival of the resurrection and a sovereign God's promise of a new life caps Lent off.

This chapter is designed to help you plan the term of Lent. But don't begin to make Sunday-by-Sunday lesson plans at this point; simply generate ideas. Later we'll begin to make explicit plans.

DRAMATIC WORSHIP IN LENT

The season of Lent provides a special time to help Christians walk more consciously with God, and worship provides a great help. In broad strokes, worship during this term moves from celebration to passion to celebration, from ecstasy to agony to ecstasy again. Here's how.

Although Easter Day is six weeks away, educational preparations should begin right at the beginning of the season by helping folks enter into Lent with attendance at the

—parish *Shrove Tuesday celebration.* This celebrative event sets us up to hear the note of pain introduced at the

—*Ash Wednesday* evening service. By building on this moment with

—a midterm, specially *instructed burial office*, we are better prepared for

—*Palm Sunday*, with its Great Procession and dramatic passion Gospel reading. The pain deepens in the events of *Holy Week*, and is given sharp focus on

—*Maundy Thursday*. In an evening liturgy the altar is stripped bare, all color is removed from the church, the candles extinguished, and the church building darkened. Following Palm Sunday's passion Gospel reading, worship on Maundy Thursday fuses together the experience of death with the Easter resurrection. By the time of the

—*Easter vigil*, the recently darkened light is clearly coming closer again, and on

—*Easter Day*, the Grand Procession that has roots six-weeks deep takes joyful shape, and both children and adults will easily understand

—*flowering a cross* and the

—decoration of an *Easter egg tree*.

Encourage the entire Sunday school to walk the walk of Lent. But remember that encouragement is better fostered by good plans than by telling folks what they "ought" to do.

POINT. An explicit program schedule, constructed especially for Lent and known by the whole parish, is the key to success in this endeavor.

Because the drama of Lent is so powerfully focused by the events of Palm Sunday and Holy Week, make special plans for this short period.

Palm Sunday's passion Gospel offers a grand opportunity for experiential education. As a dramatic reading, it can involve the entire congregation, and church publishing houses offer ready-to-use formats.

If the dramatic passion reading is used, consider constructing the liturgy using the suggestions in chapter 10 of *CEME*. Place the Gospel for the Liturgy of the Psalms as the first Gospel of the day, and save the participatory passion Gospel as one to be read after the post-communion thanksgiving and before the final hymn, as a Second Gospel reading. Then small children will have something toward which to look forward. Instead of wanting to "leave," they will be happy to wait because they expect to participate with everyone else. The final hymn might then be Herzliebster Jesu, "Ah, Holy Jesus,

How Hast Thou Offended...?" (Hymn 158 Hymnal 1982) bringing the congregation right up to the foot of the cross. This is what it's all about, isn't it?

Maundy Thursday's liturgy and the vigil of Easter follow right along.

Children are easily engaged by this approach to Christian education, and so are adults.

TOPICS AND TASKS FOR ALL AGES

With only a bit of modification, every lectionary-based curriculum easily fits into the pattern of terms proposed by *Creative Christian Education*. What results is coherence between classes and among families. Instead of a noise, a symphony develops.

1. A Bible story appointed by the lectionary is always appropriate for classroom study.

2. Two important feast days also appear:

—St. Joseph (March 19), Jesus' earthly dad, and

—the Annunciation (March 25), when Gabriel announces to Mary that she will bear a son (Luke 1:26ff).

The pain of parents when they commit themselves to the task of making a family is clearly recognized by the inclusion of Mary and Joseph in this season.

Studies for small children might look at Jesus' painful struggle from the perspective of his earthly parents, who cared so much and probably felt powerless to help. Adult studies might begin from the perspective of parental pain and continue by exploring the pain that often troubles parents today.

3. Lent also supports a study of the world's more hostile response to God and God's gospel and the more painful side of human existence. The following suggestions are just a few that might tease your interest.

a) Explore the faithful life and witness of St. Stephen, and help your children make sense of unwarranted death in God's world.

The fact is, God does not want us to abuse one another, but we are free to do so. Use the good news method of telling Bible stories to explore this topic, or use a story from everyday life as suggested in this book's chapter 9.

b) Dying and death are issues that trouble Christians of every age. With just a little help from you, these not-much-talked-about subjects can be approached in nonthreatening ways. Chapter 12 in *Creative Christian Education* suggests ten other ways to explore these important issues with small children.

c) If you or your parish decide to explore the issues of death and dying in this term of study, an instructed burial office (presented about midterm as a part of your normal pattern of Sunday worship) can offer an important perspective.

d) Within the context of this Lenten study suggestion, visit a cemetery and/or funeral home. Both are sometimes places of fear for children and adults, and curiosity will be met with answers when such visits are carefully scheduled.

e) Lent provides a perfect time to explore the risky kind of care Jesus gave to the world and what we can learn from him about the risk in providing Christian care to the world today. Six Bible stories are suggested. There are many more, and you can't possibly use them all, so pick only one or two.

f) The history of the church includes recollections about those who dared to minister in God's name in previous generations. *Creative Christian Education* suggests six as examples of a host of others.

g) Why do the righteous suffer, and if God is so good why is there destruction in the world? Tough questions deserve to be heard and addressed, and Lent provides a fine opportunity. "God's Good Friday—Today: A Study for Lent," a section in chapter 12 of *Creative Christian Education*, offers help and guidance, along with chapter 8 and 9 in *CEME*.

h) Because Easter celebrates the resurrection of Jesus from the dead, during the early generations of life in the church the egg and the butterfly came to symbolize this event. Symbols communicate what they represent. Children particularly will learn that God made us for life, not death, while making eggs or butterflies or flowering a "dead" cross with flowers on Easter Sunday morning.

i) Remember the shut-in your class adopted. Some of your plans during this term should include a way to reach out to him or her.

j) Still more classroom activities are found on page 164 of *Creative Christian Education*.

CLASSROOM POSSIBILITIES FOR PRE-SCHOOL THROUGH GRADE SEVEN

By this time it should be clear that there are more than a few possibilities available for study in Lent. Your task is to make hard decisions about what you want to focus on and why.

But in addition to the suggestions just noted, think about using the following tasks to give "action" to your explorations.

1. Use class time to prepare the Christian education bulletin board for Lent or the bulletin board to help your parish anticipate Easter. This is an expression of good pastoral care (pastoral, from the Greek *poimen*, meaning "shepherding"), an important lesson for Christians.

2. Plant a seed or bulb now for "resurrection." Use I Cor. 15:35-43, for there Paul says that "what you sow does not come to life unless it dies" and "it is sown a physical body and it is raised a spiritual body" (RSV).

Or plant flower seeds now in flats so they can be transplanted in the spring, to places around the church, on Rogation Sunday during the Easter/Pentecost term.

3. Make an Easter basket of grass seeds for the very young, and prepare to decorate the Easter egg tree with brightly colored eggs and butterflies on Easter Day.

4. How about a trip to the cemetery? Where are the persons buried who were members of our church? Now a part of the church triumphant, they are still a part of us.

5. Investigate the symbols of the butterfly and Easter egg, and learn what they communicate about God's action in the midst of life.

CLASSROOM POSSIBILITIES FOR TEENAGERS

The searching to make sense of things that characterizes the growth of adolescent Christians is met particularly well by Lent. Consider topics like these:

1. If God is so good, why do bad things happen to us? This is a question to which teens will flock, and the good news method of telling Bible stories can be used to examine God's participation in stories from the Bible and stories from everyday life. See chapters 8 and 9 in this book for helpful, practical suggestions.

2. What risks are there in daring to care for others? Women and men in the Bible and church history provide a good place to begin

this discussion, or study Jesus helping others. If you choose to study Jesus, speculate about his angry response to injustice in his day and also speculate about the angry response of the world to him. But never lecture teenagers. Always consider beginning with a story. Gently share your ideas, if necessary, but mostly encourage class discussion and identification by asking leading questions.

3. Why is fasting important, and how do people "fast" today?

4. Study the ministry of the church at the burial of the dead. What does the action of the church say about life and God's love? Why do we use a pall? Why do we sing great hymns at the burial of the dead? Schedule a trip to the funeral home.

CLASSROOM POSSIBILITIES FOR ADULTS

You can, of course, choose to continue the explorations begun in previous terms. But more is possible, and some of the same topics of interest to teens and small children might stir your ideas for adult education.

In summary, Lent provides an opportunity to do the following:

1. Pick up on themes in the story of Mary and Joseph as they "lost" Jesus following their trip to Jerusalem. Treat the pain that often troubles parents today, such as the pain caused by the struggles facing their children. How do parents offer appropriate help?

2. Explore the faithful life and witness of people like St. Stephen, and make some sense of unwarranted suffering and death in God's world. Use the good news method of telling Bible stories to explore this topic, or use a story from everyday life as suggested in this book's chapter 14.

3. Examine dying and death. The older we adults grow, the more our thinking turns toward thoughts of death and dying. Lent provides a perfect time to explore these topics.

—Take a look at the liturgy for the burial of the dead.
—Visit a funeral home.
—Prepare for one's own funeral.
—Construct a last will and testament.

Pastoral care is well served by explorations like these.

4. Explore the risky kind of care Jesus gave to the world and what we can learn from him about the risk in providing Christian care to the world today.

5. Examine the lives of those who dared to minister in God's name in previous generations.

6. Using the guidelines suggested in chapters 8 and 9 of *CEME*, explore God's good news action today even when our lives are troubled.

CHAPTER EIGHTEEN

Planning the Easter/Pentecost Term: Made by God for Life
Using *Creative Christian Education*

The Easter/Pentecost term is an eight-week celebration of Easter, so God's promise of new life is its major content and focus.

The length of this term will vary according to when you decide to end your nine-month Sunday school program. In addition, two other items will interest you.

1. Sunday morning church school is coming to a close. Expect attendance to begin to drop, so don't spend your energy fighting this normal reality. The more intensive explorations of Epiphany and Lent just won't take place this term.

2. Preregistration for next year ought to take place now. If enthusiasm has been generated all along, you'll have little trouble finding out who's going to be present next year. But this is a task not for the classroom teacher; it is the task of the Christian education committee of your governing board or the vestry.

ENJOYING WORSHIP

You may not be in a position to plan the worship in your parish, but if you see in the following some possibilities that can support your classroom teaching, most clergy will be more than happy to consider what you ask.

1. *A blessing of the animals.* The middle of May is a first-rate time to think about blessing some animals. St. Francis would like it, and so would the authors of Genesis. They charge us to be carefully responsible for all God's creatures. This kind of worship is education not to be missed, for both the young and the old.

2. *The days of rogation.* These are times to remind ourselves to take care of God's world. This important Sunday is discussed in chapter 13 of *Creative Christian Education.*

3. *The day of the Ascension.*

4. *Pentecost.* This is often called the birthday of the church, and on this day parish worship celebrates the gift of God's Spirit. Balloons and banners, grand parades, maybe a skit or play, lots of song— here's the shape of the celebration, and every class ought to contribute something to it.

5. *Mother's Day and Father's Day.* These ought not to be forgotten. Although they are not recognized as church festivals, in support of family life today they ought to be informally acknowledged with celebration.

Devote some time in class to an exploration about the ways in which moms and dads bring life to your children today.

TOPICS AND TASKS FOR ALL AGES

Choose a Bible story appointed by the lectionary to be read during this term. Six themes also provide a way to group all the stories that fall in this term's lectionary list, and each theme is expanded with suggestions for Bible stories in chapter 13 of *Creative Christian Education.*

1. *St. Paul: everyone of us.* To some degree Paul is everyone of us. From a time when he knew very little of Jesus, to a later time of intense antagonism toward the early church, to still later encounter, conversion, and growth in the early Christian community of faith, Paul's life touches the major currents that shape the hearts and minds of Christian people. When you study Paul's journey in faith, you study the walk of everyone with God.

2. *Stories of the resurrection.* After being met by Jesus, Paul's immediate reaction was to retreat, first to regain his sight and later to more deeply reflect on what happened. Still later he also began to involve himself in the early church. He heard the stories of Jesus' ministry, probably meeting face to face with people like Thomas, Mary, Peter, and Cleopas, all of whom had seen Jesus after the

resurrection. These stories and the people they include provided turning points in Paul's life.

3. *Stories of Jesus bringing life.* Besides accounts of the resurrection, in the first days of the church Christians inevitably recalled stories of Jesus' healing ministry. Paul would have loved every one of these stories, and the good news method of telling Bible stories provides a vivid way to explore them today.

4. *Parables Jesus used to explain life.* In addition to stories of the resurrection and recollections of healings, Jesus' parables would have teased St. Paul's interest.

5. *Paul builds the church.* No other term provides for the expansive exploration of Paul's conversion and ministry like this term. His enthusiastic response to the risen Christ was of such a quality that small congregations of Christians were formed throughout Asia Minor, and as far away as eastern Europe and Rome.

6. *Stories of the Good Shepherd himself.* The fourth Sunday of Easter, for Anglicans, has always been designated Good Shepherd Sunday, not officially but affectionately—sort of like the third Sunday of Advent is known as "Stir Up" Sunday because of that day's collect. Stories of the Good Shepherd are particularly appropriate for this term, especially for the very young.

It's not too late to ask your clergy to explain how visits to the sick are made. Perhaps you could join them on a Sunday afternoon visit to the hospital, or maybe take flowers from the altar. Your visit will be a ministry of good shepherding.

You should be planning a last visit to the shut-in you adopted, and this last visit will provide a grand opportunity to share some of what you studied through the year.

Say goodbye to your students, and make sure they say goodbye to one another. Try brainstorming to develop memories of the good times you have had together.

CLASSROOM POSSIBILITIES FOR PRESCHOOL THROUGH GRADE SEVEN

Stories from the Bible are always appropriate in every term, and just one will carry you a long way in six weeks. So pick a Bible story that illustrates one of the themes noted above, add to it a task or two, and you will have finished the seven or eight weeks before you know it.

1. Explore the appearances of Jesus after the resurrection. Encourage your class to wonder how people felt when they saw Jesus. How about Thomas touching Jesus' wounds as one-such story?

2. How about each class making a special class banner, to be processed on graduation day, about Jesus helping people?

3. "Good Shepherd" Sunday is always the fourth Sunday of Easter. Check the readings and collect to see why.

4. Make plans now for transplanting your plants on Rogation Sunday. Did you plant things during Lent that can be moved outside, beautifying the church building for the summer?

5. Mention the blessing of the animals sometime in May. What animals will your children bring?

6. A final visit to your shut-in will occur during this term. Prepare to visit with a party, maybe in the company of your clergy on one of their pastoral visits.

7. Take time to say good-bye to one another.

CLASSROOM POSSIBILITIES FOR TEENAGERS

Adolescent folks are always searching to make sense of things. One way to keep their interest is to meet them where they are, and the resurrection narratives meet this criteria directly.

1. Explore the appearances of Jesus after the resurrection. The Good News Method of telling Bible stories offers help.

2. Study St. Paul's conversion, he saw Jesus, too. Wonder what it was like on the road to Damascus. Think about dramatizing this event.

3. Think about dramatizing some of the events in Jesus' everyday ministry while he was still among us, and offer them to classes of younger children. These were the stories that captured the interest and formed the basis of belief in the early church.

4. Using the guidelines suggested in chapters 8 and 9 of *CEME*, explore God's good news action today in the lives of your students.

CLASSROOM POSSIBILITIES FOR ADULTS

You can choose to continue the explorations begun in previous terms. But, in addition, Bible stories from the lectionary are always of interest to Christians. They can be picked to illustrate any one of the following themes.

1. St. Paul: Everyone of Us
2. Stories of the Resurrection
3. Stories of Jesus Bringing Life
4. Parables Jesus Used to Explain Life
5. Paul Builds the Church
6. Stories of the Good Shepherd Himself
7. God's Good News Action Today (Use the guidelines suggested in chapter 9 of *CEME*)

During the year, your class may have raised questions from time to time that you did not or could not address. Now might be the perfect time for an exploration.

APPENDIX

A Bookstore for You

It need not be said in any more than one sentence: Every age group learns differently, and what works for one age group may not serve another age group well at all.

Happily, there are publishing houses across this land devoted to helping the Sunday morning teacher work with every age range. Still, many of us who teach live in or near small towns, and bookstores that stock these resources are generally not close at hand. This chapter is designed to be a small book store for you.

Over the course of several years I've discovered several books upon which I've grown to depend. This chapter lists some of them, and every one of them can be ordered through the

Virginia Seminary Book Service
Seminary Post Office
Alexandria, VA 22304
toll free telephone number: 1-800-368-3756

But if you telephone the Seminary Book Service, don't forget to mention that you are calling because of this note in *Christian Education Made Easy*. We're always trying to figure out how we can better serve Christian education in the church.

In addition, every church publishing house constructs a yearly catalog listing its titles in the field of Christian education. For many years I have used a number of the books published by Morehouse Publishing (formerly Morehouse-Barlow), and now I write for them.

You can contact them at

Morehouse Publishing
78 Danbury Road
Wilton, CT 06897
1-203-762-0721

and they will be happy to send you their most recent catalog. Other publishing houses are equally happy to help, and in all these places you will likely find all the assistance for which you are looking. Now for a list of titles.

CELEBRATING BIBLE STORIES

The Bible is full of stories, and lectionaries arrange them according to seasonal themes. But many teachers need help when exploring the "adult written" Bible with small children.

The Sunday Paper and The Sunday Paper Junior by Christian Education Resources, 19 Colony Road, New Haven, CT. 06511. These lectionary based cartoons and commentary on the ministry of teaching are authored by Gretchen Wolff Pritchard. They are particularly designed to give children something "to do" in the liturgy on Sunday morning, while also providing numerous ideas for the Sunday morning classroom teacher and ideas for discussion at the home dining table.

Several of the illustrations in *CEME* are also drawn from Gretchen Pritchard's widely acclaimed *The Sunday Paper's* Baptism Book, NEW LIFE.

Advent to Pentecost by Patricia B. Buckland (Wilton, CT: Morehouse-Barlow, 1979). Explains the origins of the church year, what it teaches, and why.

Teaching the Bible to Adults and Children by Dick Murray (Nashville, TN: Abingdon Press, 1987). The author develops ten useful strategies helpful when teaching the Bible. One will probably fit your class to a *T*.

Living the Bible With Children by Dorothy Jean Furnish (Nashville, TN: Abingdon Press, 1979). This simple-to-use book approaches the task of teaching Bible stories with an infectious enthusiasm.

Teaching the Bible: Creative Techniques for Bringing Scripture to Life by Willard A. Scofield (Valley Forge, PA: Judson Press, 1986).

Living the Good News published by the Episcopal Diocese of Colorado (P.O. Box 18345, Denver, CO 80218). Every Bible reading appointed in the Book of Common Prayer's eucharistic lectionary (as well as the psalm) is developed into a lesson plan suitable for all ages, from the very young through the adult years.

The Family Book of Bible Stories by John Britt Donovon (Wilton, CT: Morehouse-Barlow, 1986). Thirty-one Bible stories are adapted for children, with suggestions about how they can be told.

The Friendship Series (Christian Reformed Church, Grand Rapids, MI 1984). This curriculum is a bright spot in the field of classroom resources designed to involve students in the study of Bible stories. Materials include thirty sessions per year over a three-year period. Because it is written for people with mental impairments, it is carefully constructed and clearly focused. But because it is written for the mentally impaired doesn't limit its usefulness, at all, to the general church. Bible stories from both testaments are included, and classroom plans supply workable ideas for children, youth, and adults.

Arch Books, published by

Concordia Publishing House
South Jefferson Avenue
St. Louis, MO 63118
314-664-7000

These Bible stories simply told for the very young, often in verse and always with pictures. Concordia also publishes the Arch Books *in a videotape format.*

Cruden's Complete Concordance to the Old and New Testaments by Alexander M. Cruden (Grand Rapids, MI: Zondervan, 1970). Every teacher will eventually want to use a Bible verse or story but can't remember where it's found. That's where a concordance helps. There are many on the market, and Cruden's is an old friend of mine.

CRAFTS AND ACTIVITIES: GENERATING GOOD ACTION AND FOND MEMORIES

Classroom activity moves students from abstract ideas to personal knowledge. It's one thing to study about Daniel in the lion's den, and another thing to present it as a play with all its attendant activities.

The following resources offer more help than you'll be able to use.

The Banner Book by Betty Wolfe (Wilton, CT: Morehouse-Barlow, 1974). The best banner book around, filled with practical explanations and lots of suggestions. An important aid in helping your class celebrate what they are learning.

Banners for Beginners by Cory Atwood (Wilton, CT: Morehouse-Barlow, 1987).

Eyes to See God: A Book of Arts and Crafts Activities by Ann Elliott (Wilton, CT: Morehouse-Barlow, 1977). Wrapped in a few pages are a ton of ideas on such things as mobiles, dimensional pictures, collages, and more. An excellent help for the teacher who lacks a lot of craft ideas.

Bring on the Puppets by Helen S. Ferguson (Wilton, CT: Morehouse-Barlow, 1975).

The Display Book: Do-it-Yourself Display Techniques by Kerry Dexter (Wilton, CT: Morehouse-Barlow, 1977). How to make bulletin board displays that get attention.

Saints, Signs and Symbols by W. Ellwood Post (Wilton, CT: Morehouse-Barlow, 1974). If you want to know what a sign or symbol means, or what sign goes with what saint, this book not only provides a picture but briefly states factual details.

A Time of Hope by Ehlen-Miller, Miller, VanderVeen, and VanderVeen. (Wilton, CT: Morehouse-Barlow, 1979). Family celebrations and activities for Lent and Easter.

DRAMA AT ITS BEST

Drama provides rich opportunities to explore the Bible. Most all of us can remember a childhood pageant, the story it told, and our place in it, and we can feel in those memories the experience of God's love. Drama offers the same gift today, and the following resources offer all kinds of practical advice.

The Play's the Thing, How to Begin a Drama Ministry by Brian Medkeff-Rose (Nashville, TN: Abingdon Press, 1986). A how-to book that provides plenty of simple guidelines in only a few pages.

Spiritual Growth through Creative Drama, for Children and Youth by Pam Barragar (Valley Forge, PA: Judson Press, 1981). A how-to book that provides plenty of support for the notion that spiritual growth and education take powerful shape when drama is used.

Creative Drama for Senior Adults by Isabel Burger (Wilton, CT: Morehouse-Barlow, 1980). Adult education need not be simply a lecture on the Bible.

CREATING WORSHIP THAT SATISFIES

Festival worship deserves the best we educators have to offer. It is, after all, God we honor. When our worship sings with six weeks of classroom work, what results is an experience I can only describe as blessed.

In addition to chapter 6 in *Creative Christian Education* and chapter 10 in *CEME*, the following books offer practical help.

Make a Joyful Noise by James E. Hass (Wilton, CT: Morehouse-Barlow, 1973). Creative suggestions for worship on major feast days.

Symbols of Church Seasons and Days by John Bradner (Wilton, CT: Morehouse-Barlow, 1977). Festivals and seasons are arranged together.

Praise the Lord by James E. Hass (Wilton, CT: Morehouse-Barlow, 1974). Celebrations for teenagers, with opportunity for discussion and planning.

Young Children and the Eucharist by Urban Holmes (San Francisco: Harper and Row, 1982). A first-rate discussion from the late dean of the School of Theology of the University of the South.

Renewal in Worship by Michael Marshall (Wilton, CT: Morehouse-Barlow, 1985).

EPISCOPALIA: LEARNING ABOUT THE EPISCOPAL CHURCH

Every year begins afresh in September, and every new beginning is marked by new folks asking questions and old questions raised again. The All Saints and Epiphany terms both offer an important opportunity to explore denominational history and polity. Answers to questions encourage bonding and affiliation. When we don't understand and when our questions aren't answered, generally we quit. The following resources can also be used for new member classes, vehicles for incorporation increasingly being used by fast growing congregations.

An Introduction to the Episcopal Church by J.B. Bernardin (Wilton, CT: Morehouse-Barlow, 1935, 40, 57, 78, 83).

What is Anglicanism? by Urban Holmes (Wilton, CT: Morehouse-Barlow, 1982).

The Story of the Episcopal Church (Cathedral Films and Videos, P.O. Box 4029, Westlake Village, CA 91359). This resource in two parts, called a video companion to the catechism, is narrated by David Morse of "St. Elsewhere" fame.

An excellent program, it shows, in slightly less than one hour, three hundred years of Angelicanism in America. It comes with a study guide.

WORKING WITH TEENAGERS

If you are interested in working with teenagers, part II in *CEME* provides all kinds of resources. But particularly see the discussion about teenagers in chapters 3 and 4 and in the chapters that comprise part IV of *CEME*.

Widely used and excellent resources are also published by the

Zondervan Publishing House
1415 Lake Drive, SE,
Grand Rapids, Michigan 49506
616-698-6900

Their "Youth Specialties" series lists titles like *Far Out Ideas, Holiday Ideas, Way Out Ideas, Ideas for Social Action*, and *Tension Getters*. If you need practical suggestions for either your Sunday morning class or the evening youth group, you will find them here.

TOPICS FOR ADULT EDUCATION

Stories from the Bible are always appropriate for Sunday morning adult education, and so is an exploration of God's ministry in the here-and-now of everyday life. But there is also more.

Adults learn best when they need to solve a problem, whether the problem is an issue of faith or belief or how to care about aging parents or how to deal with anger.

The following books are just a few of the written resources available, and they simply show the range of topics from which you can choose. Each book can be used on Sunday morning as a basis for a discussion group or as the basis for a term course of study organized by a lead teacher.

Mid-Life Crises by William E. Hulme (Philadelphia: Westminster Press, 1980). Many adults struggle alone with the harsh transitions that life naturally brings. Sunday morning adult education can profitably address this important reality and use this book as a text for those who want to read further.

The Two-Career Marriage by G. Wade Rowatt, Jr., and Mary Jo Rowatt (Philadelphia: Westminster Press, 1980). Not often do Christians have an opportunity to talk about this issue together in community, and Sunday morning offers an excellent time.

Understanding Aging Parents by Andrew D. Lester and Judith L. Lester (Philadelphia: Westminster Press, 1980).

The Church's Ministry with Older Adults by Blain Taylor (Nashville, TN: Abingdon Press, 1984). The care of older adults is of increasing concern to their children and the church. This book provides a place to begin to study the opportunities before us.

Parents and Discipline by Herbert Wagemaker (Philadelphia: Westminster Press, 1980).

When Your Parents Divorce by William V. Arnold (Philadelphia: Westminster Press, 1980).

Learning Characteristics of Children: What to Expect in the Classroom

Sunday school teachers know their children. They know first hand that they do not teach a curriculum, they teach people. Good teaching always values the person.

KNOW YOUR CHILDREN

You will likely meet several different kinds of children (both young and old) in the Sunday morning classroom. For example, Amelia is likely to be an advanced student. Larry may be learning disabled to some degree or another. Sally is likely to have trouble with self-esteem. And Barry's behavior may be a problem looking for a solution. The following descriptions are adapted from materials used by the Brethren House Ministry (Brethren House, 6301 56th Avenue, N., St. Petersburg, FL 33709, telephone 813-544-2911), and their catalog of easy-to-use, effective, classroom tested Christian education materials is as complete as any.

To return to our discussion, we classroom teachers need to know what each of our students can do well, what they like to do, and what happens when they find things difficult. The following descriptions *of just four examples* serve to alert our interest and care.

Larry is learning disabled. As a

Child: Larry has difficulty with reading and writing. His brain sees symbols and words not in the order printed, and he is embarrassed to be called on.

Teen: Larry feels inferior, but he compensates with help.

Adult: Larry sits in the back of the room and rarely participates. He is often passive.

Larry needs to be recognized as a person who has much to offer but a person who also needs to be recognized as someone with special needs. If Larry is a child, expect parents to alert you to his needs, or, if you are concerned, ask them for assistance.

Amelia is an advanced student. Things come easily to her. As a

Child: Amelia grasps ideas quickly, she doesn't like repetition and she enjoys creative activity.

Teen: Amelia quickly sees connections and can apply theological truths to inconsistencies.

Adult: Amelia looks for depth, and should be challenged.

You will likely shower a lot of attention on Amelia. Like all children, she deserves accolades and support. But in your welcome of her, don't fail to welcome the other children or to sense their special needs.

Barry is disruptive and can quickly disable the class. As a

Child: Barry is hyperactive, he is easily distracted, and he often wants to do his own thing.

Teen: Barry uses shocking speech, he demands attention in a variety of ways, and easily exaggerates.

Adult: Barry tends to monopolize and always points out exceptions.

Barry may (often) disable your class plans, and you may be either angry in response, showering him with critical attention, or you may try to be overly positive, hoping this will help him settle down. Barry needs all the attention you can give him and more. So you may need to ask his parents or your Sunday school superintendent for a consultation. With the thirty-plus minutes we have on Sunday morning, Barry's behavior is particularly abusive to the other children. Perhaps another adult can work on special projects part of the time with Barry, helping to give him the extra attention he needs.

Sally is hampered by low self-esteem. As a

Child: Sally is hesitant to try unknown and new things, she has little confidence and she likes the security of structure.

Teen: Sally is apathetic, she sticks with peer standards (doesn't want to stand out), and she is not likely to participate in discussion.

Adult: Sally has little confidence, and she resists sharing thoughts because they may not be "good" enough.

Sally needs all the positive reinforcement you can give to her. Applaud her every action and make every effort to become her friend.

THE CHARACTERISTICS OF CHILDREN: AGE 2–14

Children under fourteen years of age have always been the primary focus of the Sunday morning Sunday school, and many of us consent to teach on Sunday morning because we love this age child.

More than a few of us already know what these children need and the way in which they learn best. But some of us do not. And we're looking for help. This appendix meets that need.

The following pages are designed to give you a place to begin to think about the needs of your children, and in just a few pages some guidelines are sketched. The discussion is not exhaustive but is meant to be illuminative and immediately helpful.

Four age ranges are presented, and the discussion centers on the energy your children bring to you and some of their special needs.

POINT. If you use these guidelines when you make your Sunday plans, class sessions are likely to measure up to your fondest hopes and expectations.

PRESCHOOL CHILDREN: AGE 2–4

—At age two, nursery children are largest dependent upon an adult. But by age four they are reaching for independence.

—They cooperatively play with one another after about three years of age and become quite cooperative with other children by age four. They are fond of their friends and tend to quarrel with them quite freely. They are growing in self-confidence, and quarreling marks this growth.

—They are beginning to understand their surroundings, complying with many of the demands made upon them. You can expect them to honor your asking them to complete simple tasks.

—They often react negatively to situations and demands (early in this period) but gradually become more able to accept necessary limitations.

—They like to take responsibility and help around the classroom.

—They like to imitate others in language, manners, and habits. This is a good time to begin to learn about Jesus and other biblical models so important in the Christian church.

—They are constantly active, but toward the end of this period they become capable of longer stretches of quiet activity.

—They show fatigue by restlessness and irritability. If they are genuinely fatigued, stop the task and let them rest. Their irritability may not have anything at all to do with the quality of your teaching.

—They are gradually learning in this period what constitutes good behavior. Help them by reminding them of simple guidelines, like saying thank you.

—At two, little assignments of responsibility are possible; by four, they can begin taking some definite responsibility.

—They tend to like creative things, like dancing, singing, and playing imaginative games.

—They like to have stories read and told to them.

—They enjoy playing with blocks, crayons, paints, and clay.

—They tend to want to do more than they are capable of doing.

—Two- and three-year-olds are interested in manipulating materials just for the sake of activity; four-year-olds begin to want to make something definite.

—Boys and girls enjoy playing together because their interests are similar at this age.

—Nursery children have great curiosity and ask countless questions.

—They are beginning to understand time, morning, afternoon, yesterday, tomorrow.

—In the early part of the period, they have no ability or capacity to share—"It's mine!" By the end of the period, they are able to "take turns."

—At this age level they are not ready for competition in any field.

—They are unable to fully distinguish between truth and untruth.

Special needs:

—They need the security of love and affection from their parents.

—They need positive guidance and a pattern of behavior to follow.

—They need to experience time, patience, understanding, and genuine interest from adults.

—They need simple, clear routines with limited choices.

—They should have the opportunity to learn to give and take and to play cooperatively with other children.

—They need to widen the scope of their activity and, by the end of the period, limited freedom to move about and away from their immediate home surroundings.

—They need to have adequate opportunities to learn about their world through actually seeing and doing things themselves.

Reading to preschoolers:

1. Practice reading the story out loud (if you have time), to hear what your voice sounds like. Become familiar with it. It is easier to hold their attention when you don't have to read every word and so keep looking at the book and not the children.

2. Be sure to read the story slowly; preschoolers need time to hear, look, and understand.

3. Hold the book so that they all can see the pages. Turn the pages slowly. Try holding the book slightly to one side of you, so that you look down and across to read it, but the book faces the children. Hold the book firmly with one hand, and with the other turn the pages or point to things on the page as you talk about them or as the children ask questions.

4. Vary your voice with the mood of the story; don't be afraid to make up the voices and act out the parts.

5. Try to keep an eye on the children to see how they are reacting. If they seem very disinterested it might be a good idea to cut the story short.

6. Children should be seated comfortably an informally—the floor is a good spot and can, if needed, be covered by cushions, mats, or rug samples. Make sure they have lots of elbow room. *Preschoolers are wigglers.* Their wiggling does not necessarily mean loss of attention, just their tremendous energy. You should expect it and accept it—just make sure that everyone has plenty of room.

7. To help the children settle down to listen to the story, try telling them something about it briefly—you may introduce the characters or have a simple song or fingerplay that relates in some way to the story you are going to read.

8. Don't dig for reactions to the story. Their expressions and how attentive they are will tell you how they liked it. However, if they ask questions, listen and try to answer. Use the opportunity to expand on the subject; it could be the beginning of art projects or a play or games.

9. Give them a chance to look at the book you read if they want to and at any others you may have. Teach them to care for them but, most of all, to enjoy them.

PRIMARY CHILDREN: AGE 5-8

—They are capable of little abstract thought and learn best through active participation and concrete situations.

—They find enjoyment in songs, rhythms, fairy tales, myths, nature stories, true stories, comics, radio, movies, and television. By the end of the period, they become interested in collections and adventure stories.

—They are continuing in their growth from dependence to independence.

—They are capable of taking more responsibility but are often prone to "forget." They still need some adult supervision.

—They are learning how to work through group plans and to cooperate with members of the group with which they work.

—They demand their own turn and their own rights and make much of "fairness."

—They are becoming competitive and like to make rules both for themselves and others.

—They are able to understand safety precautions but may "forget" or be overly daring, especially toward the end of the period.

—They freely express their feelings about adults and resent being told what to do—"too bossy," "not fair."

—Their ability and accuracy are increasing.

—They are eager and curious about almost everything. They have a real desire to learn.

—They are growing from primary interest in present and immediate reality to interest in the past, too.

—They want and need adult approval of their actions.

—Boys and girls still play together, but differences in plans and interests are becoming marked.

—They are more interested in the activity at hand than in the end result of the activity.

—They are capable of spontaneous dramatization and carry on simple classroom dramatization well and with imagination.

—They are moving from dependence on approval of adults to the beginning of dependence on the approval of their peers.

—They are becoming more able to evaluate themselves accurately. Hence, they are anxious to do well.

—They are developing a growing understanding of time and of the use of money.

—They are concerned about problems of "right" and "wrong."

—They are eager and are inclined to show more enthusiasm than wisdom.

—They are full of energy but are inclined to tire rather easily; they are restless and often appear dreamy and absorbed.

Special needs:

—They need encouragement, ample praise, warmth, and great patience from adults.

—They need the right combination of independence and encouraging support.

—Wise guidance should be provided, channeling their interests and enthusiasms *rather than dominating* them and being overly critical in the assignment of standards for their behavior.

—They should have ample opportunity for activity of many kinds, especially for the use of their large muscles.

—Concrete learning situations and active direct participation are musts in the classroom for this age level.

—They must learn to make adjustment to rougher ways of the playground. They need adult help to do this without becoming too crude or rough or being overwhelmed by the problem.

—They should be given some responsibilities, though without pressure and without being required to make extensive decisions or to achieve rigidly set standards.

—They need acceptance at their own level of development, with an understanding of their specific nature and interests.

—They need help in the gradual development of acceptable manners and habits.

—They need friends and, by the end of the period, a "best friend."

JUNIOR CHILDREN: AGE 9–11

—They are showing greater responsibility, dependability, reasonableness, and have developed a strong sense of right and wrong not characterized in the younger age levels.

—Their individuality is becoming distinct and clear. Wide discrepancies in their ability and interests are appearing.

—They are capable of prolonged interest and often make plans that carry over a fairly long period of time. They often tend to go ahead on their own initiative.

—Their interests center strongly in "gangs" of one sex only, which are of short duration and changing membership. This trend is stronger among the boys than among the girls. Girls tend to relate to two or three good friends.

—They are perfectionistic, want to do well, but lose interest easily if discouraged or pressured.

—They are less interested in fairy tales and fantasy, and more interested in stories about boys and girls, science, adventure, and the world about them. They understand the relation of past, present, and future.

—They have a great feeling of loyalty to their church and much pride in it. Many are acolytes, choir members, and occasional ushers.

—Much of their time is spent in talk and discussion, and they are often outspoken and critical of adults, although they are still dependent upon adults for approval. They argue over fairness in games and the making of rules.

—Their friendships often break up because of different rates of maturing, resulting in different interests. Children in this age group, nearing puberty, need different programs from those children who are still immature.

—At this age, differences are appearing in the interests of boys and girls, some antagonizing and teasing goes on between them.

—They are often overactive, hurried, and careless because of high energy level. They are prone to have accidents.

—They are learning to cooperate somewhat better and take an active part in group planning and activities, though they are still reluctant to give up their own wishes. They do a great deal of arguing in developing plans.

Special needs:

—They need active, rough-and-tumble play for the development of their whole body.

—They need to have friends and membership in a group.

—They should have organized club and group activities provided for their use.

—Opportunity for training in skills without pressure should be available to them.

—They should have some expectation in the area of responsibility. Opportunities to take responsibility and make plans with adult support and guidance at difficult points is very desirable. Parish worship is a great asset for their growing sense of responsibility.

—They need reasonable explanations, should not be "talked down to." They like a chance to talk things over.

—They should have opportunities to have their questions answered.

—They should have continued wise guidance and channeling of their interests and enthusiasms with *warm understanding, affection,* and support from their family group. They want to feel that they are an important, useful member of the family.

—They need opportunities for creativity through *art, music, rhythm, dramatics,* and similar activities.

—They need help in learning to get along with others and to accept those who are different from themselves.

—They need help in learning how to meet competition.

INTERMEDIATE CHILDREN: AGE 12–14

—They seek acceptance by their age-mates (peers).

—Their gangs continue, though loyalty to the gang is still stronger among boys than girls.

—Sometimes there is a great deal of teasing and seeming antagonism between boy and girl groups.

—Those of this age group who are maturing begin to show some interest in the other sex.

—They are interested in team games, outdoor activities, pets, hobbies, collections, radio, television, comics, movies, and activities to earn money. The interest of boys and girls is diverging.

—They may become moody, overcritical, changeable, rebellious, and uncooperative.

—The opinion of their own group is beginning to be valued more highly than that of adults.

—They can work cooperatively on teams and in groups. There is a strong emphasis on fairness and on rules.

—They are self-conscious about their body changes.

Special needs:

—They need varied programs to meet different maturity needs.

—Organized group activities based on boys' and girls' needs and interests should be provided.

—They need help in understanding the physical and emotional changes beginning to take place.

—They need warm affection and a *sense of humor* in adults— *no nagging, scolding,* or *talking down.*

—They need a sense of belonging and acceptance by their peer group.

—Opportunities for boys and girls to do things together in group activities are needed.

—Opportunities should be provided for greater independence and for carrying more responsibility, but still without pressure.

APPENDIX C